STUDIES IN THE ENGLISH RENAISSANCE

John T. Shawcross,
General Editor

THE
MILTONIC
MOMENT

J. Martin Evans

THE UNIVERSITY PRESS OF KENTUCKY

Publication of this volume was made possible in part by a grant from the National Endowment for the Humanities.

Editorial and Sales Offices: The University Press of Kentucky
663 South Limestone Street, Lexington, Kentucky 40508-4008

02 01 00 99 98   5 4 3 2 1

Frontispiece: Giottodi Bondone, The Test of Fire
before the Sultan. S. Croce, Florence, Italy

Library of Congress Cataloging-in-Publication Data

Evans, J. Martin (John Martin), 1935-
    The Miltonic moment / J. Martin Evans.
        p.   cm. — (Studies in the English Renaissance)
    Includes bibliographical references and index.
    ISBN 0-8131-2060-8 (acid-free paper)
    1. Milton, John, 1608-1674—Criticism and interpretation.
    2. Milton, John, 1608-1674. On the morning of Christ's nativity.
    3. Milton, John, 1608-1674. Lycidas. 4. Milton, John, 1608-1674.
    Comus. 5. Renaissance—England. I. Title. II. Series.
    PR3588.E9   1998
    821'.4—dc21   97-53104

For Mariella

CONTENTS

PREFACE

> One of the central problems facing a student of Milton today is how to interpret what he wrote between 1628 [*sic*], the year of his *Ode on the Morning of Christ's Nativity*, and 1641, when the first of his excitedly reformist pamphlets appeared.
>
> —Annabel Patterson, *John Milton*, 10

IT HAS NOW BEEN JUST OVER FORTY YEARS since Rosemond Tuve published her magisterial study of the images and themes in five of Milton's shorter poems. With the exception of J.B. Leishman's *Milton's Minor Poems* (1969) and C.W.R.D. Moseley's *The Poetic Birth: Milton's Poems of 1645* (1991) most subsequent analyses of these texts have treated them separately in individual articles or monographs. By doing so, they may have unintentionally distracted us from what I believe to be one of the most distinctive qualities of Milton's early work—its unity. Reading almost any of the poems that eventually found their way into the volume of 1645, one is struck over and over again by their extraordinary interconnectedness, by the almost organic way in which they lead into and out of each other, so that each segment of the total corpus simultaneously looks forward to its successors and backward to its predecessors. We are normally accustomed to think of poems as discrete entities, but Milton's insist on being read in relationship to each other. Just as he deliberately violated the traditional division between octave and sestet in the sonnet on his blindness, so Milton seems to have been consciously challenging the conventional boundaries that separate one poetic text from another. For example, with its modified rhyme royal stanza and its tribute to a child who will "stand 'twixt us and our deserved smart" (69) *On the Death of a Fair Infant Dying of a Cough* reads like a prologue to the *Nativity Ode;* in the opening stanza of the *The Passion,* Milton begins by remembering his celebration of the "joyous news of heav'nly Infant's birth" (3) in the *Ode;* the lilting tetrameters of Comus's hymn to "Tipsy dance and Jollity" (104) echo both the rhythms and the sentiments of *L'Allegro* no less clearly than the sombre arguments of *Il Penseroso* try to contradict them; and the first line of *Lycidas* invites us to remember every poem Milton had ever written before 1637. To a greater degree than that of any other English poet, perhaps, Milton's early poetry is all of a piece. To treat any single component of it in isolation is to run the risk of mistaking a part for a whole.

There is a second and still more fundamental way in which these texts can be said to constitute an organically unified body of work, however: they all share a distinctive *gestalt,* a common perceptual and cognitive structure that differentiates them from almost any other poetry being written in the 1620s and 1630s. Although I shall necessarily be concerned with the intratextual relations these early poems establish both to each other and to the rest of the Miltonic corpus, then, my principal concern will be to identify and describe a recurring mental pattern that identifies them as the cultural products of a particular literary intelligence operating at a particular religious and political juncture in the history of seventeenth-century England. Many of the points I will be making in the following pages will also have relevance to Milton's major works, and from time to time I shall undoubtedly find myself drawing upon them to illustrate a specific point, but the unique character of Milton's vision presents itself with exceptional clarity and freshness in the poems he composed at the beginning of his literary career. My discussion will focus, therefore, on three representative examples of his early work: *On the Morning of Christ's Nativity* (1629), *A Mask performed at Ludlow Castle* (1634), and *Lycidas* (1637). Between them, these three texts not only provide an example of each of the three principal genres in which Milton worked as a young man—ode, masque, and elegy—but taken together they encompass a complete human life from birth, through the experience of moral struggle, to death. Yet different as they are both generically and thematically, all three poems exemplify the characteristic mode of apprehending and representing human experience that I call "the Miltonic moment."

THIS BOOK IS THE PRODUCT of thirty four years of teaching and research at Stanford University. During the course of its preparation I received helpful comments and advice from numerous students, friends and colleagues, and in particular from John Bender, Seth Lerer, Marjorie Perloff, and John Rumrich, who read earlier drafts of several chapters. I am also grateful to the anonymous readers for Kentucky University Press who made many useful suggestions, and to my research assistant, G. E. Light, who helped me prepare an earlier version of the manuscript. Finally, I would like to record my gratitude to: Medieval Texts and Studies for permission to incorporate material from my article "A Poem of Absences," which originally appeared in *Milton Quarterly* 27 (1993) 31-35; to the English Department of the University of Victoria for permission to reproduce parts of my monograph "The Road From Horton," which was published in the *English Literary Studies* monograph series in 1983, and to the Susquehanna University Press for permission to include an expanded version of an article "From Temperance to Abstinence: The Argument of *Comus* Revisited," which I contributed to Charles W. Durham and Kristin P. McColgan (eds.) *"All in All": Unity, Diversity, and the Miltonic Perspective* (Selinsgrove: Susquehanna University Press, 1998).

ABBREVIATIONS

Note: All quotations from Milton's prose and poetry are from the Columbia edition of the complete works.

CE	*College English*
CQ	*Critical Quarterly*
CW	*The Works of John Milton*
ELH	*Journal of English Literary History*
HLQ	*Huntington Library Quarterly*
JEGP	*Journal of English and Germanic Philology*
MLN	*Modern Language Notes*
MLQ	*Modern Language Quarterly*
MLR	*Modern Language Review*
MP	*Modern Philology*
MQ	*Milton Quarterly*
MS	*Milton Studies*
NQ	*Notes and Queries*
PBSA	*Publications of the Bibliographical Society of America*
PMLA	*Publications of the Modern Language Association*
QQ	*Queen's Quarterly*
RES	*Review of English Studies*
SEL	*Studies in English Literature*
SP	*Studies in Philology*
SRen	*Studies in the Renaissance*
TSLL	*Texas Studies in Language and Literature*
UTQ	*University of Toronto Quarterly*

Introduction

THE MILTONIC MOMENT

What we call the beginning is often the end
And to make an end is to make a beginning.
The end is where we start from.
                    —T.S. Eliot, *Little Gidding*, 216-18

"THE MOST SIGNIFICANT THING in all his work," Ruskin once
wrote of Giotto, "is his choice of moments." Faced with the task
of illustrating the life of any Christian figure, the painter always
singled out the "decisive instant" in the story, the turning point of
the entire narrative. In his fresco of St. Francis's trial by fire on
the wall of the Bardi Chapel in Santa Croce, Florence, for in-
stance, Giotto focused on the moment at which the Sultan is actu-
ally in the process of abandoning paganism for Christianity. The
saint stands on the very brink of the flames, but he has not yet
entered them. Sensing their impending defeat, the heathen Magi
are ready to slink away in disgrace, but they have not yet left the
scene. As the Sultan himself gazes at his former advisers "with
quiet eyes of decision," the spiritual balance is clearly just about to
shift. But for this single brief instant everything is frozen in a state
of suspended animation.[1] In the words of a more recent art critic,
Giotto's compositions "capture the action at the culminating point,
which is very often the precise moment at which the representa-
tion may also hint at what has gone before and suggest the prob-
able outcome."[2]

   Milton's choice of moments is equally significant, and for
many of the same reasons. Like Giotto, Milton always seems to
concentrate on the "decisive instant," the narrative juncture at

which the climactic sequence of events is just about to happen. And since it is clear that these events will almost invariably take the story in a new direction, the Miltonic moment is always pivotal, a moment of crisis that takes place immediately before the plot undergoes a dramatic change of course. Milton's poems consequently look both backward and forward, backward to a past that is about to be superseded or repudiated, forward to a future that will begin to unfold as soon as the poem is over. In William Kerrigan's words, they "imitate moments of historical density—something in past time comes to an end, something in future time begins to appear."[3] The Miltonic moment occurs between an end and a beginning.

To take a concrete example, in what may well have been his first original poem, the *Carmina Elegiaca*, composed while he was still a student at St. Paul's School, Milton dramatizes the daily human experience that most closely corresponds to the kind of narrative crux I have been attempting to define: the experience of waking up. Like the closely related prose theme on rising early, written at about the same time, this Latin school exercise takes place in the liminal zone separating unconsciousness from consciousness, the fleeting interval when we are neither fast asleep nor wide awake. Until the poem's opening words have been uttered, the person to whom they are addressed has been sunk in "unwarlike slumber" (14): "Arise, come, arise; now it is time, put an end to easy slumbers. The light is born, leave the foot of the languid couch" (1-2). One by one the sleeper's senses gradually come back to life, beginning with the sense of hearing: "Now crows the sentinel bird, the cock, herald of the sun, and wakeful calls each man to his business" (3-4). Then the sense of sight becomes aware of the rising sun: "The flame-bearing Titan puts forth his head from the waves of the East, and spreads his shining radiance over the happy fields" (5-6). And finally, the sense of smell begins to respond to the stimuli of the freshly opened flowers: "Now the wild rose breathes fragrant odors, now violets smell sweet, and the corn rejoices" (9-10).[4] By this point in the poem the nameless sleeper is almost awake, so the speaker urges him to compare the delights of the external world with the dreams and sorrows of his "feeble slumbers" (13-17). The speaker concludes by repeating his opening command: "Arise, come, arise; now it is time, put an end to easy slumbers. The light is born, leave the foot of the languid couch" (19-20). The process of waking up, one senses, is complete; the unconscious figure to whom these words were originally addressed is now fully alert, ready to begin the day's work.

In its carefully limited focus on the transition from one condition to its opposite this little school exercise seems to me to be paradigmatic of Milton's entire poetic output, and not least of the three poems with which I shall be principally concerned in this study. All three, we may begin by noting, commence with an act of recollection. The *Nativity Ode* looks back in its opening stanza not only to the birth of the Christ child but to the era that immediately preceded it:

> This is the Month, and this the happy morn
> Wherein the Son of Heav'n's eternal King,
> Of wedded Maid and Virgin Mother born,
> Our great redemption from above did bring;
> For so the holy sages once did sing,
> That he our deadly forfeit should release,
> And with his Father work us a perpetual peace. [1-7]

No sooner does the poet begin to celebrate the coming of the Messiah than he reminds us of the Old Testament prophets who had foretold his miraculous birth. Our "great redemption" is the fulfillment of a promise that was given long before. In *Comus* the initial retrospect is strictly narrative. The Earl of Bridgewater, the Attendant Spirit informs us, has recently been appointed Lord President of Wales, and his children are on their way to Ludlow Castle "to attend their Father's state / And new-entrusted Scepter" (35-36). Their path, however, will take them through an "ominous Wood" (61) where the son of Circe and Bacchus lies in wait to tempt them with

> His orient Liquor in a Crystal Glass,
> To quench the drouth of Phoebus, which as they taste
> (For most do taste through fond intemperate thirst)
> Soon as the Potion works, their human count'nance,

Th'express resemblance of the gods is chang'd
Into som brutish form of Woolf, or Bear,
Or Ounce, or Tiger, Hog, or bearded Goat,
All other parts remaining as they were. [65-72]

The forthcoming action will be a kind of rite of passage, a test that "most" prior travelers have failed but that the Lady and her brothers must pass before they can proceed on to the festivities honoring their father. The opening lines of *Lycidas*, on the other hand, link the forthcoming lament not to any earlier incidents in the history of Cambridge University or the life of Edward King but rather to the literary biography of the poem's author: "Yet once more, 0 ye laurels, and once more / Ye Myrtles brown, with Ivy never sere, / I come to pluck your Berries harsh and crude" (1-3). The elegy is simply the most recent in a chain of repeated exercises in premature poetic utterance by John Milton. As we begin to read it, we are being asked to remember everything that the poet has written so far.

And just as they begin by looking back, so Milton's poems usually end by looking forward. Indeed, nothing is more characteristic of his works than their open-endedness. To quote Kerrigan again, they are "curiously anticipatory and, in a special way, incomplete."[5] So though the *Nativity Ode* seems to conclude at nightfall, in reality a new dawn is about to break; the Christ child is about to embark on his redemptive mission. Like the sleeper in the *Carmina Elegiaca*, the world is about to begin a new day. In *Comus*, too, the apparent closure of journey's end at Ludlow Castle gives way almost immediately to the prospect of another, still more arduous pilgrimage to a destination "higher than the Spheary chime" (1020), while in *Lycidas*, even as the sun is setting, the shepherd who sang the poem is rising to prepare himself for another day in "fresh Woods and Pastures new" (193).

Situated as they are between a retrospective beginning and a prospective conclusion, most of Milton's poems consequently communicate a profound sense of immediacy. They typically take place not then and there but here and now, before our very eyes. More often than not, this intense *presentness* is created by the poet's favorite mode of address, the dramatic monologue, which he uses in the *Carmina Elegiaca*, in *On the Death of a Fair Infant*, in *L'Allegro*, in *Il Penseroso*, and in *Lycidas*, to name only the most obvious instances. But even when Milton adopts a narratorial stance, as he does in the opening stanza of the *Nativity Ode*, he structures the poem in such a way that by the time we come to the end of it the voice (or, as I shall argue later, the voices) singing the hymn seems to be physically present at the manger in Bethlehem: "But see, the Virgin blest / Hath laid her Babe to rest. / Time is our tedious song should here have ending" (237-39). The narrative distance between the present in which the poem is being performed and the past in which the events it describes took place has all but disappeared. And the spectators who witnessed the original production of *Comus* must have had a very similar feeling, for to a greater degree than any other seventeenth-century masque Milton's tribute to the Earl of Bridgewater is relentlessly local and contemporaneous in its setting. The Lady and her brothers are impersonating themselves in a drama that is set at the very time (September 29, 1634) and in the very place (Ludlow) where the audience itself is located. The conventional gap between the world of the play and the world of the playgoer has been totally obliterated, with the result that at the end of the masque the earl and his guests can join his children in their "victorious dance" (974) without crossing the barrier of the footlights. Fiction and reality have coalesced completely.

At the same time, however, the pivotal nature of the Miltonic moment also communicates a powerful sense of *inter*mediacy. The poems seem to take place between the boundaries that separate one event, or one series of events, from another; they occur, as it were, between the acts—*in mediis rebus*—outside the normal course of everyday experience. In the case of the *Nativity Ode*, for instance, history is temporarily suspended as the poem begins; the sun literally stands still, and the poem unfolds in a kind of extratemporal interim until, at the end of the final stanza, the frozen tableau at the manger is about to come back to life again. In *Comus* the sense of intermediacy is primarily narrative; the Lady's adventures are an interruption in her journey to Ludlow Castle, an unwelcome hiatus in a progressive movement toward celebration and reunion. And in *Lycidas* both temporal and narrative continuities are interrupted, as the elegy insists on its own status as a mere interval by beginning in the dramatic present and then, in the final lines, projecting both the singer and his song backward into an undefined narrative past.

To anyone familiar with Patricia Parker's study of narrative deferral in *Inescapable Romance,* this account of the intermediacy of the Miltonic moment may well seem analogous to "the element of 'betweenness'" that she discovers in *Paradise Lost.* But the phenomenon I am describing here differs in at least one crucial respect from the "threshold of decision" that Parker analyzes so acutely. For unlike Adam and Eve in the state of innocence, or Hercules at the crossroads, the consciousness that experiences the Miltonic moment is faced not so much with an impending choice as with a radically new mode of being, not so much with a fork in the road as with a sharp bend. The "betweenness" Parker explores, that is to say, resides in a "pivotal or pendant zone" between two polar opposites—good and evil, light and dark, life and death.[6] The "betweenness" I shall be attempting to define resides in a temporal interstice between two events, or two sequences of events, on a chronological continuum.

This recurrent sense of intermediacy in Milton's early works corresponds in turn to three quite specific historical circumstances that shaped both the poet's private and public worlds. To begin at the purely personal level, while he was writing these poems Milton was himself experiencing a period of temporary suspension at his parents' home, first in London and then in Hammersmith and Horton. The *Nativity Ode* was composed during the Christmas holidays, when the poet was briefly removed from the ongoing current of academic life in Cambridge, while *Comus* and *Lycidas* were composed during the extended intermission that took place between Milton's departure from the university in 1632 and his voyage to Europe in 1638. All three poems are, in a sense, "vacation exercises," written in the intervals separating different phases of their author's life. To a greater or lesser extent, they are themselves pivotal events in Milton's biography.

No less significantly, perhaps, all three poems were written during the eleven years' tyranny, when all parliamentary activity had been brought to a standstill by Charles I's dissolution of the

House of Commons in 1629. The decade during which Milton composed much of his early poetry was thus a period of political suspension, as it were, a prolonged and widely resented interruption in the normal process of Britain's parliamentary governance. Whether or not he was as radically inclined during these years as Michael Wilding and David Norbrook have suggested,[7] Milton surely must have felt that he was living through an enforced interlude in the political life of the nation. The sense of intermediacy that characterizes so many of his early poems may well reflect the widespread feeling that the period of the "king's peace" constituted a temporary parenthesis in the narrative of Britain's historical evolution, an interparliamentary hiatus that, sooner or later, must inevitably come to an end.

On a still larger scale, it is also worth bearing in mind that the first half of the seventeenth century witnessed an unusually sustained outbreak of millenarian speculation. As Christopher Hill, David Loewenstein, and David Norbrook have recently reminded us, the most violent explosion of millenarian publications took place in the early 1640s in the wake of the Puritan revolution, but the movement as a whole had its roots much earlier in the century.[8] Indeed, ever since the late 1500s scholars and theologians such as John Napier had been calculating the precise date of the second coming, and many of them had come to the conclusion that "this is even the last houre, the world cannot continue long."[9] An English translation of Thomas Brightman's *A Revelation of the Revelation* (1609), with its vision of England as the protagonist of the apocalyptic drama, was published in 1611, 1615, and again in 1644, and Joseph Mede's scholarly *Clavis Apocalyptica*, with its prophecy that the fall of Anti-Christ would be complete within a quarter of a century, appeared in print in 1627.[10] Thanks to these works and others like them, a sense of imminent cosmic renovation gripped many Englishmen during the period in which Milton was composing the *Nativity Ode*, *Comus*, and *Lycidas*. A characteristic passage from Brightman's treatise may suggest something of the prevailing mood. "Nowe is the last Act begun," he wrote, "of a most longe & dolefull Tragedy, which shall wholy overflowe with scourges, slaughters, destructions, but after this Theater is once removed, there shall come . . . a most delightfull spectacle of perpetuall peace, joined with abundance of all good thinges."[11] So when Milton declared in 1641 that "thy Kingdome is now at hand, and thou standing at the dore," he was giving voice to an idea that had been current for at least the previous decade or so.[12] With its powerful implications of an impending dénouement, then, the Miltonic moment is the narrative equivalent of the widely held belief that the world was on the brink of the millennium.

Another way of putting all this would be to say that the Miltonic moment is essentially transitional, and as a matter of fact the poems under consideration here are all about transition in one form or another: from paganism to Christianity in the *Nativity Ode*, from youthful inexperience to moral maturity in *Comus*, from pastoral retirement to heroic engagement in *Lycidas*. In each case the poem itself is a record of the peripeteia, and in at least one case is its instrument. The fundamental operation that these works perform, then, is change. As I demonstrate, they not only contain a number of individual metamorphoses—Christ's exchange of "that glorious Form" (8) for a "darksome House of mortal Clay" (14) in the *Nativity Ode*, the Attendant Spirit's disguise as Thyrsis and Sabrina's "quick immortal change" (841) in *Comus*, and Edward King's apotheosis as "the Genius of the shore" (183) in *Lycidas*— but they also enact the process of transformation.[13]

As in the case of Giotto's fresco in the Bardi Chapel, finally, this transformation is often ideological as well as historical or biographical. Almost invariably, the narrative reversal is accompanied by a shift from one system of belief to another, as if Milton were constantly attempting to reenact the process of conversion. Indeed, in chapter 1 I argue that the *Nativity Ode* is nothing less than a prolonged meditation on the physical, moral, spiritual, and literary consequences of the Christian experience of regeneration. In chapter 2 I investigate the parallel transition in *Comus* from the classical ethic of temperance, with its emphasis on the inherent goodness of the natural world and the moral self-sufficiency of the human individual, to the Christian ethic of chastity, with its polarized view of the postlapsarian world and its insistence on the moral dependence of fallen human beings upon the grace of God. And in chapter 3 I offer an interpretation of *Lycidas* as the record of Milton's personal decision to abandon a life of contemplative pastoral retirement for an active career of erotic and political engagement.

This last point raises once again, of course, the much debated issue of Milton's political stance in the years preceding the Puritan revolution. David Norbrook believes that "Milton's early poetry is radical not only in its explicit political comments but in its underlying visionary utopianism," while Michael Wilding is convinced that the poetry of the 1630s exhibits "unmistakable assertions of revolutionary sentiments" in such long-neglected phenomena as Comus's references to "capitalistic wealth-accumulation" and "mass exploitation" during his great speech on Nature's fertility and Milton's "recognition and sympathy for the labouring class" in his portrayal of the shepherds in the *Nativity Ode* and *L'Allegro*.[14] I would locate the radicalism of these poems less in such specific textual details than in the more general structural features that they all share. For with their continual emphasis on transformation, their profound sense of imminence, and their concluding visions of a resolutely activist future, whether it be the ministry of Christ in the *Nativity Ode*, the ascent to "the palace of eternity" in *Comus*, or simply the commitment to a new kind of life in *Lycidas*, these early poems all implicitly predict that, sooner rather than later, the political and religious intermission through which Milton and his contemporaries believed they were living will come to an end, that the course of their personal or national histories is about to follow a new and dramatically different trajectory. From the very beginning, one could say without exaggeration, the Miltonic moment was a moment of revolution.

1

THE POETRY OF ABSENCE

It is in the significant silences of a text, in its gaps and absences, that the presence of ideology can be most positively felt. It is these silences which the critic must make 'speak.'

—Terry Eagleton,
Marxism and Literary Criticism, 34-35

IN AN INFLUENTIAL ARTICLE published in 1940, Arthur E. Barker argued that the *Nativity Ode* records an experience in Milton's life "which corresponds to the conversion of his Puritan associates."[1] Amplifying on Barker's point, A.S.P. Woodhouse claimed two years later that "taken together, the *Nativity Ode* and *How Soon Hath Time* give evidence of an experience that stands to Milton in place of what the Puritans called conversion."[2] Despite Rosemond Tuve's cautions against "over-personal" readings of the poem, this view of the *Ode* as "the testimony of Milton's religious experience" has gained wide currency in more recent critical discussions.[3] According to Patrick J. Cullen, for instance, the *Nativity Ode* "is structured so that the meditator himself experiences a conversion from pagan illusion to the new Christian truth of the babe in the manger."[4] In much the same vein, I.S. MacLaren argues that the poem enacts "the process by which the narrator gradually perceives the significance of both God's offer of grace through the Son and man's responsibility for response entailed in that offer."[5] And Georgia Christopher defines Milton's subject as "the revolution that grace makes in the consciousness of the poet."[6]

All these readings of the poem as a kind of confessional autobiography seem to me to be based upon a patently false assumption, namely, that there is an individualized human presence in the text to be converted—whether Cullen's "meditator," MacLaren's "narrator," or Christopher's "poet." In fact, I want to argue, the *Nativity Ode* is the most rigorously depersonalized of all Milton's nondramatic works. It is a poem that faces not inward but outward, a poem that casts the reader rather than the poet in the role of the convert.

To begin with, the very form in which Milton chose to compose his poem militates against an autobiographical interpretation. For whether we follow Robert Shafer, George N. Shuster, Carol Maddison, and Paul H. Fry in identifying the poem as an ode, or Philip Rollinson in reading it as a hymn, the genre of the *Nativity Ode* automatically implies a choric rather than an individual speaker.[7] In the performance of Pindar's odes, Shafer reminds us, "the chant of the chorus still held undisputed the place of first importance," while the hymn, Fry remarks, is almost by definition "a choir-poem that harmoniously effaces the individual."[8] Sensitive as he always was to generic expectations, Milton created accordingly a voice that is essentially choric in nature. As the final lines of the proem make clear, the "hymn" (17) is sung by the heavenly muse in concert with "the Angel Quire"—hence the insistently plural pronouns in the latter part of the poem: "our" ears, "our" senses, "our" fancy, "our" song (126, 127, 134, 239).[9] Far from belonging to an individualized poet or his surrogate, the voice we hear performing the "humble ode" (24) is public rather than private, communal rather than personal, celestial rather than human.[10]

In this respect, it is instructive to compare the *Nativity Ode* with its intended companion piece, *The Passion*. The latter poem is almost literally suffocated by the poet's self-consciousness:

> Befriend me night best Patroness of grief,
> Over the Pole thy thickest mantle throw,
> And work my flatter'd fancy to belief,
> That Heaven and Earth are colour'd with my wo;
> My sorrows are too dark for day to know:
> The leaves should all be black whereon I write,
> And letters where my tears have washt a wannish white.
> [29-35]

During the course of this one stanza, Milton refers to himself no less than six times, and the poem as a whole is obsessively self-referential. The *Nativity Ode*, on the contrary, contains not a single "I," "me," or "my" in its thirty-one stanzas. If *Lycidas* is "a poem nearly anonymous," in John Crowe Ransom's famous formulation, the *Nativity Ode* comes as close as a poem can to being wholly anonymous.[11]

This lack of personal involvement stands out in marked contrast to most literary representatives of the Nativity tradition. If we compare the *Nativity Ode* with almost any other celebration of Christ's birth written in the sixteenth or seventeenth centuries, what strikes us immediately is the absence of any reference in Milton's poem to the effect of Christ's birth upon the poet himself. At the end of "New Heaven, New Warre," for example, Robert Southwell turns from the manger scene to exhort his own soul to remain loyal to his savior:

> My soul with Christ join thou in fight,
> Stick to the tents that he hath dight;
> Within his crib is surest ward,
> This little babe will be thy guard;
> If thou wilt foil thy foes with joy,
> Then flit not from the heavenly boy. [43-48]

In the sestet of his sonnet on the Nativity, John Donne, after addressing the Christ child throughout the octave, suddenly shifts his attention to his personal spiritual concerns:

> Seest thou, my soule, with thy faiths eyes how he
> Which fills all place, yet none holds him doth lye?
> Was not his pity towards thee wondrous high,
> That would have need to be pittied by thee?
> Kisse him, and with him into Egypt goe,
> With his kinde mother, who partakes thy woe. [9-14]

And in similar vein, Ben Jonson, in the concluding lines of "A hymne on the Nativitie of my Saviour," meditates upon the significance for himself and his readers of the events he has just described:

> What comfort by him doe wee winne,
> Who made himselfe the price of sinne
> To make us heires of glory.
> To see this babe, all innocence:
> A martyr borne in our defence;
> Can man forget this storie? [19-24]

There is nothing even remotely corresponding to these sentiments in the *Nativity Ode;* the poem does not contain anyone who could experience them.

The presence of a poet or his surrogate in the text of a poem does not, of course, depend exclusively upon the use of the first-person pronoun. It can also be implied by a direct, second-person address to the reader or to the subject of the poem. Thus, in the sestet of his sonnet on "Christmas," George Herbert suddenly abandons his narrative stance in order to pray to the child whose birth he has been describing:

> O Thou, whose glorious yet contracted light,
> Wrapt in nights mantle, stole into a manger;
> Since my dark soul and brutish is thy right,
> To Man of all beasts be not thou a stranger:
> Furnish and deck my soul, that thou mayst have
> A better lodging than a rack or grave. [9-14]

And Henry Vaughan, after celebrating Christ's birth and its impact on the natural world, devotes the final two stanzas of "Christ's Nativity" to informing the child of his own inadequacy and sinfulness:

> I would I had in my best part
> Fit rooms for thee, or that my heart
> Were so clean as
> Thy manger was,
> But I am all filth, and obscene,
> Yet if thou wilt thou canst make clean. [19-25]

Milton, on the contrary, never addresses the child directly.

Jesus is consistently referred to in the third person: "Nature in awe to him" (32), "He her fears to cease" (45), "His raign of peace" (63). As a result, there is nothing in the *Nativity Ode* to parallel the agonized yearnings of Herbert or Vaughan for personal regeneration. It is difficult, therefore, to agree with Barker when he claims that the effects of the experience recorded in the poem "correspond in general to the effects of the puritan conversion," for there is no one in the poem to register those effects.[12] In one of the most original articles on the *Nativity Ode* to appear in the last ten years, Richard Halpern argues that, by "putting off epic expansiveness to dwell in the 'humble ode,'" Milton enacts a *kenosis* or "emptying out" analogous to "Christ's decision to forego heaven and lie 'meanly wrapt in the rude manger'."[13] My point is that "Milton's parallel *kenosis*," as Halpern calls it, is rather more radical: he has effectively erased himself from his own poem.

At first sight, this lack of any subjective presence might seem strange in the work of a Puritan poet, who might normally be expected to dwell at length on his own spiritual response to Christ's redemptive mission, but I believe it is part of an overall strategy that is quintessentially Puritan. We may begin by noting that though the poet is the most notable absentee, he is by no means the only one. For whereas most representations of the Nativity in art and literature focus on the presence of the wise men and the shepherds at the manger, Milton sets the scene before their arrival. The Magi are still on their way to Bethlehem:

> See how from far upon the Eastern rode
> The Star-led Wisards haste with odours sweet,
> O run, prevent them with thy humble ode,
> And lay it lowly at his blessed feet;
> Have thou the honour first, thy Lord to greet. [22-26]

And the shepherds are still in the fields with their flocks: "The Shepherds on the Lawn / Or ere the point of dawn, / Sate simply chatting in a rustic row" (85-87). The heavenly muse has "prevented" them all. When we encounter the child in the manger, there is no one standing between us.

What is more, Mary and Joseph have been effectively banished from their traditional positions. The former eventually makes a brief appearance in the final stanza; the latter never appears at all. As Blake failed to notice when he illustrated the poem, the only figures we encounter in the early stanzas are the personified abstractions of Nature, Peace, Truth, Justice, and Mercy.[14] The entire scene, one could say without exaggeration, has been completely dehumanized. The space that in so many Nativity representations was crowded with observers is totally empty. Even the traditional ox and ass have been expunged. The *Nativity Ode* is truly a poem of absences.

Milton's strategy of erasure is too consistent to be accidental. It reflects, I believe, the characteristically Puritan distaste for allowing any intermediary to intrude between the individual soul and its Maker. By purging the scene of all the traditional witnesses of the Nativity, Milton forces the reader to respond to the scene not vicariously, through the experience of the wise men and the shepherds, but directly. Nobody, not even the poet, stands between the reader and the babe in the manger. To a greater extent than in any other Nativity poem, we encounter the Christ child face to face.

As Lowry Nelson has noted, moreover, Milton heightens this sense of immediacy by collapsing the tenses of the poem in such a way that the events seem to be taking place in a kind of timeless present, both then and now.[15] From the opening stanza of the hymn onward, the verbs alternate between past and present so frequently—"was" (29), "lies" (31), "was" (35), "woo's" (38), "Sent" (46), "strikes" (52)—that the narrative finally seems to transcend chronology. We are simultaneously looking back at the Nativity across history and witnessing it as it happens. "This is the month and this the happy morn."

Seen in such a temporal context, Milton's choice of moments has theological as well as structural significance. For the narrative is organized so that, though the child has been born when the poem begins, he has not yet been welcomed or accepted by the world. The induction insists that the sky, "by the Suns team untrod, / Hath took no print of the approaching light" (19-20). Literally, of course, this description establishes the fact that the scene takes place just before sunrise. Metaphorically, however, it suggests that the world is still "untrod" by the Son, that the "approaching light" of Christ has not yet risen. Like the anonymous sleeper at the beginning of the *Carmina Elegiaca*, the human race is only on the verge of waking up to a new reality. As the first witnesses of the Nativity, the poem thus implies, we too have yet to be illuminated by the arrival of the Savior. Together with Nature, in the opening stanzas of the "Hymn," we are unregenerate, unenlightened, still trapped in a pre-Christian stage of our history. The shepherds' lack of awareness that the "mighty Pan" has "kindly come to live with them below" (89-90) interprets retrospectively our position as we start reading; our "silly thoughts" (92), too, are preoccupied with other matters.

In a sense, then, one might say that the *Nativity Ode* is about the *reader's* conversion, the *reader's* dawning awareness of the new birth and its overwhelming consequences. By creating a spatial and temporal vacuum between his audience and the "Heav'n-born childe" (30), Milton draws them into the poem no less surely than he transforms the spectators of *A Mask Performed at Ludlow Castle* into participants in the Lady's adventures. Like the women of Canterbury in T.S. Eliot's *Murder in the Cathedral*, they are forced to bear witness, to experience as if for the first time the effects of the redeemer's birth. My disagreement with Barker thus has to do not so much with the nature of the experience recorded in the poem as with its location. If indeed a personal conversion takes place during the course of the *Nativity Ode*, it is the reader's, not the poet's. As Catherine Belsey has put it, Milton's celebration of the "infant God" (16) is "a redemptive text," an evangelical speech-act.[16]

The conversion that the poem describes, however, is far broader in scope than the illumination of any individual human consciousness. For Milton is concerned here with nothing less than the transformation of the entire universe. Christ's entry into our "darksom House of mortal Clay" (14) brings about a cosmic revolution after which nothing will ever be the same again. Beginning with the banishment of the pagan gods from their earthly shrines in Greece, Rome, Syria, and Egypt, the course of history now leads inexorably towards the apocalyptic moment when "Time will run back and fetch the age of gold" (135) and "Heav'n as at some festivall, / Will open wide the Gates of her high Palace Hall" (147-48). In order to treat a theme of such magnitude, Milton's imagination turned almost inevitably to the great classical description of universal regeneration, Virgil's fourth *Eclogue*, where he found a vivid account of the successive changes in the natural environment initiated by the birth of a miraculous child, "under whom the iron brood shall first cease, and a golden race spring up throughout the world."[17] As many critics have noted, the resemblances between the *Nativity Ode* and *Eclogue IV* are numerous. Not only do both poems describe the transformation of the world by a baby bearing, in Virgil's phrase, "the gift of divine life" (15), but also both insist that this transformation was prophesied by earlier seers (the Sibyl of Cumae in the *Eclogue* and the "holy sages" (5) of the Old Testament in the *Ode*); both portray the descent of a virgin goddess (Astraea in the *Eclogue* and the biblical virtue of justice and her sisters in the *Ode*), whose arrival on earth signals the return of the golden age; and, most important of all, both offer similar analyses of the way in which the renovation of the earth and its inhabitants will be accomplished.

According to the *Eclogue*, the process will be a gradual one, with three quite distinct stages. During the first stage, when the child is still in its infancy, the natural world will begin to revert to its original state of perfection; the earth will produce plants without cultivation, the animals will no longer prey on one another, and both the animal and the vegetable kingdoms will become wholly benign: "For thee, child, shall the earth untilled pour forth, as her first pretty gifts, straggling ivy with foxglove everywhere, and the Egyptian bean blended with the smiling acanthus. Uncalled, the goats shall bring home their udders swollen with milk, and the herds shall not fear huge lions; unasked, thy cradle shall pour forth flowers for thy delight. The serpent, too, shall perish, and the false poison-plant shall perish" (18-25).

But only the physical environment will be affected by this initial set of changes; human nature will still retain its destructive and sinful impulses. So during the second stage, when the child is old enough to read, mankind will repeat its violent history despite the burgeoning abundance of nature: "But as soon as thou canst read of the glories of heroes and thy father's deeds, and canst know what valour is, slowly shall the plain yellow with the waving corn. ... Yet shall some few traces of olden sin lurk behind, to call men to essay the sea in ships, to gird towns with walls, and to cleave the earth with furrows. A second Tiphys shall then arise, and a second Argo to carry chosen heroes; a second warfare, too, shall there be, and again shall a great Achilles be sent to Troy" (26-36).

During the third and final stage, when the child has grown into a mature man, the world will become so fertile that it will no longer be necessary for men to labor, compete, or trade for goods. Every nation will be materially self-sufficient and the arts of civilization will disappear: "Next, when now the strength of years has made thee man, even the trader shall quit the sea, nor shall the ship of pine exchange wares; every land shall bear all fruits. The sturdy ploughman, too, shall now loose his oxen from the yoke. Wool shall no more learn to counterfeit varied hues, but of himself the ram in the meadows shall change his fleece, now to sweetly blushing purple, now to a saffron yellow; of its own will shall scarlet clothe the grazing lambs" (37-45).

In the *Nativity Ode*, too, nature's transformation takes place in three clearly differentiated stages, though their characteristics are rather different from those in Virgil's account. As in the *Eclogue*, the initial stage restores peace and harmony to the world, but in Milton's version of the phenomenon human as well as natural conflict is suspended:

> No war, or Battels sound
> Was heard the World around
>   The idle Spear and Shield were high up hung,
> The hooked Chariot stood
> Unstain'd with hostile blood,
>   The Trumpet spake not to the armed throng,
> And Kings sate still with awfull eye,
> As if they surely knew their sovran Lord was by. [53-60]

The second stage consequently focuses not on the ongoing violence of the human race but rather on the supernatural repercussions of the infant's birth: the cessation of the pagan oracles that begins on "this happy day" (167), Christ's redemptive agony on the cross, and the day of judgement:

> With such a horrid clang
> As on mount Sinai rang
>   While the red fire, and smouldring clouds out brake:
> The aged Earth aghast
> With terrour of that blast,
>   Shall from the surface to the center shake;
> When at the worlds last session,
> The dreadful Judge in middle Air shall spread his throne.
> [157-64]

The third stage, when "our bliss" (165) is finally consummated, consists of a cosmic version of Virgil's pastoral idyll. In place of the material prosperity described in the *Eclogue*, Milton offers us a world without sin and a universe without hell. The multicolored sheep of the classical poem give way to the daughters of God:

> Yea, Truth and Justice then
> Will down return to men,
>   Orb'd in a Rain-bow; and like glories wearing
> Mercy will sit between,
> Thron'd in Celestiall sheen,
>   With radiant feet the tissued clouds down stearing,
> And Heav'n as at som festivall,
> Will open wide the Gates of her high Palace Hall. [141-48]

Like Virgil, then, Milton insists that the birth of the miraculous child is only the beginning of a long and painful process that will not be completed until "the world's last session" (163). Just as the second quest for the golden fleece and the second siege of Troy must precede the arrival of the golden age in *Eclogue IV*, so here the cessation of the oracles, the crucifixion, and the day of judgement must all take place before "our bliss / Full and certain is" (165-66).

The real significance of Milton's adaptation of Virgil's account of nature's conversion lies, however, not so much in the various points of resemblance or difference between the two texts as in the act of adaptation itself. According to most commentators, this act is essentially corrective in nature. E.K. Rand, for instance, remarks that, in order "to match the Pagan's Messianic prophecy, [Milton] has written a pastoral Birth Song for the real Messiah, in which Christian purity and truth dispense with the gaudy trim of Pagan imagery."[18] And the author of a more recent analysis of Milton's debt to *Eclogue IV* concludes that, "just as pagan old-epic heroism gives way to new-epic Christian heroism in *Paradise Lost*, so in the *Nativity Ode* the old pagan prophecy gives way to the new Christian prophecy and promise."[19] The *Nativity Ode* has thus come to be seen as a Christian substitute for Virgil's poem, a revision of the classical text in which the misconceptions and falsifications of the pagan worldview have been rigorously corrected in the light of Puritan orthodoxy.

In fact, the relationship between the two works is rather more complicated than that, for in the very process of reforming his ancient model Milton necessarily gives it fresh life. The *Nativity Ode* does not cancel out the fourth *Eclogue;* it regenerates it. The classical framework is not totally dismantled and abandoned; it is adjusted and modified to meet the demands of a new ideology. By rewriting the heathen text, Milton is engaged, in short, in a form of cultural conversion. In the poet's evangelical imagination, the old literature is being transformed into the new. Conversion is not simply the subject of the ode; it is the action that it implicitly performs, not only at the personal level, as I have suggested, but at the cultural level as well.

As Rand's reference to Virgil's "Messianic prophecy" may serve to remind us, Milton was by no means the first reader of the fourth *Eclogue* to find in it a premonition of the Christian nativity. Indeed, from the fourth century on, the poem had been read as a divinely inspired prediction of the biblical Messiah. Initiated by the Emperor Constantine, this hermeneutical tradition asserted that the birth of Christ had been prophesied not only by the prophets of the Old Testament but also by such Roman seers as the Sibyl at Cumae.[20] In Augustine's words, "There were also prophets not of God himself, and even in them are to be found some things which they have heard and uttered concerning Christ. So it is said of the Sibyl among others; which I would not readily believe but that a certain one of the poets, the most famous in the Roman tongue, before saying of the renewal of the age things which seem to fit with the Kingdom of our Lord Jesus Christ, prefixed a verse in which he says, 'The last age of the Cumaean song is come.'"[21] Hence the famous episode in Dante's *Commedia* when the Roman poet Statius thanks Virgil for guiding him to Christ by proclaiming the incarnation in lines 5-7 of *Eclogue IV*:

> You were as one who, walking in the night,
> Carries the lamp behind him, serving not
> Himself but teaching those who follow him,
> When you proclaimed "The world is made anew,
> Justice and mankind's primal age return,
> And from the heavens descends new progeny."
> You made me poet, you led me to Christ.[22]

Nor was this reading of *Eclogue IV* as a Christian prophecy confined to the Middle Ages. In 1628, just a year before the composition of the *Nativity Ode*, William Lisle published an English version of Lodovicus Vives's *In Bucolica Vergilii Interpretatio, Potissimum Allegorica* under the title *Virgil's Eclogues Translated into English*. In his introduction to *Eclogue IV*, Lisle noted that "Lodovicus Vives affirmeth in his Glosse upon this Eclogue that all heerein must of necessity bee spoken of Christ, to whom (saith he) I will apply the interpretation. . . . Let prophane men therefore heerein bee silent, for even in the very simple and naturall sense of the words, without any neede of Glosse or Allegory, it cannot bee understood, whatsoever is here spoken, but onely of Christ."[23] In case anyone should fail to get the point, Vives nevertheless provided a detailed commentary on Virgil's text, during the course of which he explained that the virgin who would return with the age of Saturn was the Virgin Mary, the new progeny who would descend from the heavens could only be Christ himself, and the description of the forthcoming golden age was in fact a prophecy of "the course of Christ's church, that is, his Kingdome here on earth."[24] Read in this light, the *Nativity Ode* could well be described as a text that explores the theme of conversion to the third power. It is a poetic conversion of a pagan poem about natural conversion that has itself already undergone an interpretive conversion to Christianity.

The messianic reading of *Eclogue IV* is, of course, only one example of what for a long time was the church's principal strategy for converting not only the literature but the entire cultural tradition of the ancient world, the strategy of inclusion, as I shall call it. Over and over again, the various myths and legends of classical Greece and Rome came to be interpreted as dim pagan intuitions of ideas, events, or characters described in Holy Scripture. The myth of Deucalion, for instance, corresponded to the Old Testament story of the flood; the story of Nisus paralleled the history of Samson; and the legend of Orpheus's search for Eurydice foreshadowed Christ's harrowing of hell. "Who doth not see," asked Milton's contemporary, Giles Fletcher,

> drown'd in Deucalion's name
> When earth his men and sea had lost his shore,
> Old Noah; and in Nisus lock, the fame
> Of Samson yet alive; and long before
> In Phaethon's mine own fall I deplore;
> But he that conquered hell, to fetch again
> His virgin widow by a serpent slain
> Another Orpheus was than dreaming poets feign.[25]

Read in this way, a significant portion of the old stories could be assimilated within the framework of orthodox Christian ideology, and, as D.C. Allen, Douglas Bush, and others have shown, the literature of the Middle Ages and the Renaissance is full of Christianized versions of Greek and Roman texts.[26]

Perhaps the most obvious examples of this strategy in the *Nativity Ode* are the associations of Christ first with the pagan deity Pan (89) and later with the infant Hercules (227-28). Like Fletcher's Orpheus, these two figures from classical mythology are converted into precursors of the Christian redeemer. But on a far larger scale, the entire poem enacts the strategy of inclusion, for, as we have seen, Milton's tribute to the Christ child implicitly converts Virgil's fourth *Eclogue* into a prophecy of the Nativity. In the *Nativity Ode* a Christian way of rereading Virgil's poem has become a Christian way of rewriting it; exegesis has given way to praxis.

The important thing to note here is that in both cases the underlying purpose is recuperative. Faced with the product of an alien culture, Milton and his Christian predecessors have incorporated it into the fabric of their own religious tradition by transforming it, whether through interpretation or adaptation, into an essentially new work. Far from rejecting or suppressing the classical text, they have converted it into a Christian one. The *Eclogue* is still visible, at least in outline, but it has experienced a metamorphosis so radical that it has acquired as it were a fresh identity; in Milton's hands it has become, quite literally, a new poem.

Inclusion, however, was not the only strategy that the church developed for dealing with the literary products of the classical world. Rather than attempting to co-opt them, it occasionally chose to exclude them altogether from the Christian tradition, either by banning their reproduction and distribution or by excising them from the educational curriculum. Thanks largely to the influence of such scholars as Cassiodorus, the church was somewhat reluctant to pursue the "strategy of exclusion" during the first few centuries of its history—to cut itself off from its cultural roots in Greece and Rome involved too many risks while it was still seeking to establish itself as the dominant religion in western Europe. But by the Renaissance its position was sufficiently secure to make the wholesale repudiation of classical literature a practical possibility. What is more, the distinctive culture of the period provided a powerful theoretical underpinning for such a project. For wherever one looks in the literary, political, religious, or scientific practice of sixteenth or seventeenth century England, one encounters the assumption that the way to achieve regeneration is to expel corruption. Indeed, the English Renaissance might well be called the age of catharsis.

Perhaps the best known advocate of this strategy was William Prynne, the author of *Histriomastix*, but the period as a whole is full of examples in a variety of areas. In the plays of Shakespeare, for instance, political or social renewal is almost invariably achieved by an act of banishment. The characters who represent a threat to the new order are not usually reformed; they are expelled. The rejection of Falstaff at the end of *Henry IV*, part 2, the exclusion of Shylock, Malvolio, and Don John from the reconciliations at the ends of the comedies, the banishments of Bolingbroke, Norfolk, Gloucester and Cordelia, all reflect the same basic belief: the body politic can only be restored to health by purging it of its refractory elements.

In much the same way, English colonial policy was based on the premise that most of the social and economic ills that afflicted Elizabethan and Jacobean England could be solved by deporting her least desirable citizens to the New World. In a sermon preached to the Honorable Company of the Virginian Plantation in 1622, for instance, John Donne compared the English colony to "a spleen, to drain the ill humours of the body."[27] "This course well observed and continued two or three yeeres," declared Richard Eburne in a promotional tract, "would so purge the Land of evill weeds, as Galen never better purged his diseased Patients."[28] Other promoters of England's colonial activities were even more graphic in their accounts of the purgative process. According to Samuel Purchas, the colonists were "Englands excrements" and Virginia "a Port Exquiline for such as by ordure or vomit were by good order and physicke worthy to be evacuated from this Body." Without such a purge, he argued, the body politic "either breeds matter for the pestilence and other Epidemicall Diseases, or at least for Dearth, Famine, Disorders, Ouer-burthening the wealthier, oppressing the poorer, disquieting both themselves and others, that I mention not the fatall hand of the Hangman."[29] In the popular view, lamented John White, colonies were regarded as the "Emunctories or sinckes of States; to drayne away their filth."[30] As such passages reveal, America was perceived by many Renaissance Englishmen as an enormous receptacle into which the nation's malcontents, criminals, dissenters and heretics could conveniently be discharged.

By the same token, both parties to the religious controversy of the period were convinced that the church could be reformed merely by purging it of its subversive elements. Whether the writers were Anglican followers of Archbishop Laud, urging the ejection of Puritan lecturers and ministers from the pulpit, or Puritan apologists, advocating the abolition of the ritual and doctrinal vestiges of popery, the fundamental assumption was that the ecclesiastical institutions of England could be purified by being purged. Only remove the Anglicans or the Puritans, as the case might be, and the church would be restored to health, just as the body could be healed by the favorite cure of the period: bleeding.

Against this background Christopher Kendrick is able to make a persuasive case that the expulsion of the pagan deities in the last section of the *Nativity Ode* amounts to a Puritan call to arms: "The Elizabethan compromise is behind us, and idolatry accordingly outdated; the kingdom requires cleansing; full-scale reformation is again the order of the day."[31] On a smaller scale, one might also argue, the individual consciousness requires cleansing too, and in this context the exclusions I noted at the beginning of this chapter begin to take on fresh significance. For the elimination of Joseph and Mary, the ox and the ass, the wise men and the shepherds, and even the poet himself from the "rude manger" (31) not only reflects the Puritan distrust of intermediaries, as I suggested earlier, but also purges the scene of any entity that might possibly contaminate the sanctity of the occasion. The site of the reader's encounter with the savior, one might say, has been comprehensively sterilized.

The literary tradition that most clearly exemplifies the strategy of exclusion, however, is the one that Kendrick discusses: the cessation of the oracles, according to which Christ's entry into the world brought about the pagan gods' departure from their shrines. The history of this tradition from its roots in Plutarch's *On the Cessation of Oracles* to its culmination in *Paradise Regained* has been studied in detail by C.A. Patrides, and I do not propose to repeat his observations here.[32] For the purposes of my argument, the important point to note is that in its fully developed form the immediate effect of the tradition was to exclude the pagan oracles from the body of Christian revelation. With the coming of Christ, wrote Prudentius in the fourth century, "the cavern of Delphi has fallen silent, its oracles condemned; no longer does the cauldron

direct responses from the tripod. No longer does a priest pos-
sessed utter with foaming mouth and panting breath fates drawn
from Sibylline books. Lying Dodona has lost its maddening
vapours." Far from announcing the coming of Christ, as in the
messianic reinterpretation of Virgil's fourth *Eclogue*, "Cumae is
dumb and mourns for its dead oracles."[33]

Drawing either directly on Prudentius' poem or, as Herbert
Grierson and John Carey have suggested, on Tasso's elaboration of
the story in "Nel Giorno della Nativita," Milton made this legend
the basis of the closing stanzas of the *Nativity Ode*.[34] Like Prudentius,
he identifies Apollo's shrine at Delphi and the home of Hammon in
Libya as representatives of Greek and Middle Eastern religion re-
spectively, though, in order perhaps to avoid a direct conflict with
the messianic interpretation of *Eclogue IV*, he substitutes the lars and
lemures for the sibyl of Cumae as the Roman representatives. Like
Tasso, he also describes the plight of the nymphs and the departure
of Apis and Anubis. And in order to make the banishment of the
pagan gods still more comprehensive, he adds Peor, Baalim, Dagon,
Ashtaroth, Thammuz, and Moloch.

The two interpretive traditions within which Milton situ-
ated his poem are thus radically contradictory. The Virgilian tra-
dition incorporates pagan prophecy into the structure of Chris-
tian history; the Prudentian tradition rejects it altogether. At the
very heart of the *Nativity Ode*, it might therefore appear, there lies
a profound contradiction. In the course of imitating a poem that,
in the view of the Christian church, legitimated at least one of the
pagan oracles, Milton has introduced a legend the whole point of
which was to negate them. The strategy of inclusion and the strat-
egy of exclusion coexist within the same work.

The key to resolving this contradiction, I believe, is to be found in
the structure of the conversion process itself. According to A.D.
Nock, conversion may be defined as a "reorientation of the soul
of an individual, his deliberate turning from indifference or from
an earlier form of piety to another, a turning that implies a con-
sciousness that a great change is involved, that the old was wrong
and the new is right."[35] In the rather broader sense in which I am
using the term here, it consists of a revolution, a transformation,

whether spiritual, moral, physical, or exegetical, from one condition to another, profoundly different one. The first condition is assumed to be so far inferior to the second that the transition from one to the other can take on the characteristics of a second birth or regeneration, and as a result the converted are often described as being "born again" or, in William James's phrase, "twice born."[36]

At the personal level, the classic model of conversion is the experience of Saul on the road to Damascus, but the analytical language that came to be associated with conversion derives chiefly from Paul's epistles to the Ephesians and Colossians, in which the apostle urged his readers to "put off . . . the old man, which is corrupt according to the deceitful lusts, and be renewed in the spirit of your mind: And . . . put on the new man, which after God is created in righteousness and true holiness."[37] Although Christianity produced many other accounts of conversion over the course of the following centuries—St. Augustine's experience in the garden, for instance, and Luther's in the tower—the original Pauline formulations were clearly still dominant when Milton came to compose his definition of the phenomenon in *De Doctrina Christiana*. Conversion, or, as he called it, regeneration, "is that change operated by the Word and the Spirit, whereby the old man being destroyed, the inward man is regenerated by God after his own image, in all the faculties of his mind, insomuch that he becomes as it were a new creature, and the whole man is sanctified both in body and soul, for the service of God, and the performance of good works."[38] For Milton, as for Paul, personal conversion was thus a two-stage process. First came the death of the old man; then and only then could the birth of the new man take place.

The obvious problem with this description has to do with the relationship between the two men. To put it as simply as possible, in what sense, if any, are the old man and the new man the same person? What has Saul to do with Paul? Is the regenerate man a completely new self, totally independent of the old? Is the transformation so all-encompassing that a completely different identity has been created? And what does it mean to say that the old man has been destroyed when, as countless works from Augustine's *Confessions* to Bunyan's *Pilgrim's Progress* attest, the new man is haunted by the memory of his past sins? That Milton was aware of such difficulties is suggested by the distinction he draws in the passage above between the "old man" and "the inward man." The latter seems to be a kind of neutral connecting link between the unregenerate and regenerate selves, as if the destruction of the convert's sinful nature (the old man) left behind a morally inert residue (the inward man), which is subsequently transformed by the operation of divine grace into "*as it were* a new creature." The old man, Milton seems to be implying, is not the whole man, only his corrupt and sinful components. Once those components have been obliterated, there still remains a part of him to be regenerated.

At the cultural level, the same difficulties arose when the recently converted nations of Europe were faced with the problem of coming to terms with their pagan past. In what sense were the Italy of Pope Gregory the Great, say, and the Italy of Julius Caesar the same culture? Perhaps the most succinct formulation of the problem was provided by the Christian theologian Tertullian at the turn of the second century. "What," he asked, "has Athens to do with Jerusalem?" And he was echoed by Jerome two centuries later: "What has Horace to do with the Psalter, or Virgil with the Gospels, or Cicero with the Apostle?"[39] How, in other words, was the Christian church to deal with the morally and ideologically alien literature, art, and philosophy of the ancient world? As we have seen, one obvious answer was to reinterpret the cultural products of Greece and Rome in such a way that they became ideologically acceptable to a Christian reader—the strategy of inclusion. Another was to declare that the pagan past was dead and gone, and to prohibit Christians from studying it—the strategy of exclusion.

From a theological point of view, however, neither strategy was altogether satisfactory. Practiced in isolation, the strategy of inclusion, for instance, could well be taken to suggest that evil was the raw material of good, that good was made out of evil, a conclusion that some critics have found reflected in the dynamics of *Paradise Lost*.[40] And the implications of the strategy of exclusion were even more disturbing. For if the state, the church, or the individual self could be regenerated merely by an act of purgation, then it clearly followed that the pure had always coexisted with the corrupt, the virtuous with the wicked, the healthy with the diseased. If the process of producing gold by refining away the dross was an accurate model of conversion, then the new man had always been intermingled with the old. To be saved he simply needed to be liberated from his wicked *alter ego*. The Fall, it followed, had not destroyed Adam's original integrity, as Luther and Calvin had insisted; it had merely contaminated it with sin.

Nor was Milton himself totally immune to these implications. In a fascinating discussion of revolutionary change in *The Reason of Church Government*, he argued that "if we look but on the nature of elementall and mixt things, we know they cannot suffer any change of one kind or quality into another without the struggl of contrarieties. And in things artificiall, seldome any elegance is wrought without a superfluous wast and refuse in the transaction. No Marble statue can be politely carv'd, no fair edifice built without almost as much rubbish and sweeping. Insomuch that even in the spirituall conflict of S. Paul's conversion there fell scales from his eyes that were not perceav'd before."[41] Once the excess marble has been removed from the block, the statue imprisoned inside will appear in all its purity; once the superfluous waste and refuse of the old man has been swept away, the new man will be revealed. All that is required is the act of separation. Evil, it thus appears, is extrinsic to the world, a foreign element to be purged away like the impurities of the English church. Good, by the same token, is the pure residue that is left, like gold, when all the corrupt excrescences have been expelled.

A more satisfactory answer to the problem posed by pagan culture was provided by Augustine in his *De Doctrina Christiana*. In a simile that was to become one of the great commonplaces of the Middle Ages, he proposed that Christianity should adopt all that was best in the pagan tradition just as the children of Israel had carried off and used the gold and silver vessels of their enemy during the exodus from Egypt:

> If those who are called philosophers, especially the
> Platonists, have said things which are indeed true and
> are well accommodated to our faith, they should not be

feared; rather, what they have said should be taken from them as from unjust possessors and converted to our use. Just as the Egyptians had not only idols . . . which the people of Israel detested and avoided, so also they had vases and ornaments of gold and silver and clothing which the Israelites took with them secretly when they fled, as if to put them to a better use. . . . In the same way all the teachings of the pagans contain not only simulated and superstitious imaginings . . . which each one of us leaving the society of pagans under the leadership of Christ ought to abominate and avoid, but also liberal disciplines more suited to the uses of truth, and some most useful precepts concerning morals. Even some truths concerning the worship of one God are discovered among them.[42]

Augustine's simile is important because, like Milton's definition of conversion, it preserves a certain degree of continuity between the old condition and the new. The children of Israel do not abandon Egyptian civilization in its entirety in order to make a fresh start, nor do they attempt to convert all the cultural products of Egypt to their own use—the idols are left behind. Before the exodus takes place, the Israelites perform as it were a salvage operation, rejecting the offensive elements in their old environment but preserving the potentially useful ones. Just as Milton's purified "inward man" provided the raw material that could be converted into the "new man," so the gold and silver vases and ornaments that the Israelites chose to take with them could subsequently be "put to a better use" in the Holy Land.

Seen in this context, the coexistence of both the strategy of inclusion and the strategy of exclusion in the *Nativity Ode* was inevitable if the poem was to present a comprehensive account of conversion. In the Miltonic definition of regeneration as in the Augustinian analysis of cultural transformation, both strategies were indispensable components of the process as a whole. The death of falsehood and wickedness was the necessary prelude to the birth of truth and goodness; the birth of truth and goodness was the necessary sequel to the death of falsehood and wickedness. Neither, on its own, constituted a complete conversion.

Yet despite the presence of both the strategy of inclusion and the strategy of exclusion in the text of the *Nativity Ode*, there is no denying the overwhelming prominence that Milton gives to the latter. To begin with, whereas Virgil's *Eclogue IV* offered a progressive description of nature's gradual metamorphosis, culminating in the return of the golden age, the *Ode* reverses the order in which we experience the last two stages of the sequence. After the preliminary description of universal peace, that is to say, we encounter not the expulsion of corruption (the structural equivalent of Virgil's *priscae vestigia fraudis* (31)), but the return of the golden age:

> For if such holy Song
> Enwrap our fancy long,
>   Time will run back and fetch the age of gold,
> . . . .
> Yea Truth and Justice then
> Will down return to men,
>   Orb'd in a Rain-bow; and like glories wearing
> Mercy will sit between,
> Thron'd in Celestial sheen
>   With radiant feet the tissued clouds down stearing,
> And Heav'n as at some festivall,
> Will open wide the Gates of her high Palace Hall. [133-48]

Then, just as the New Jerusalem is about to come into full view, the angels' rapture and the vision it precipitates is cut short: "But wisest Fate sayes no, / This must not yet be so" (149-50). The vision, it turns out, is premature. First, the initial process of exclusion must be completed: the pagan gods must be driven out of their shrines, the old man must be "crucified with [Christ], that the body of sin might be destroyed,"[43] and finally the damned must be separated from the elect at the Day of Judgement. In the history of the human race, as in the life of the individual human being, conversion is a lifelong operation rather than an instantaneous transformation. "We do not put off the old man in one day," wrote Calvin, "we are converted to God gradually, and by sure degrees."[44] So just as the new man will not emerge until the long-drawn-out death of the old man has run its course, so the New Jerusalem will not emerge until the oracles have ceased and the Crucifixion and Judgement have taken place. Renovation cannot begin until the process of purgation has been completed. In the description of the original act of creation in *Paradise Lost*, the Spirit of God

> downward purg'd
> The black tartareous cold Infernal dregs
> Adverse to life: then founded, then conglob'd
> Like things to like, . . .
> And Earth self ballanc't on her center hung. [7.237-42]

A similar procedure seems to be necessary in order to renovate the earth here in the *Nativity Ode*. Before it can be redeemed, the world must first be purged of its impurities in a global act of exorcism.

Milton's drastic modification of the sequence of events in *Eclogue IV* has been interpreted in a variety of ways by modern critics. George W. Smith, for example, suggests that it is an instance of what he calls "Milton's method of mistakes." The mistake in this case is made by Nature, which wrongly believes that "such harmony alone" (107) is capable of restoring the age of gold, that the redemption of the world will come about immediately "through the power of music rather than of Christ." "Wisest Fate" must intervene in order to emphasize the crucial role that the son of man will play in our salvation.[45] Patrick Cullen, on the other hand, believes that the mistake is the speaker's. Falling prey to the pagan conception of time as a cyclical process, "the meditator of the poem wrongly expects the golden age to return immediately." Fate's intervention is necessary to remind him that "the gates to the old Eden are closed. The Christ-child brings a new Eden and a new promise."[46]

Neither interpretation accurately describes the real effect of Milton's maneuver. It is extremely doubtful, for instance, whether the phrase "such harmony alone" is really intended to exclude the power of Christ, as Smith claims. What Nature "knew" (107) was the simple fact that only the celestial harmony of the angels, as opposed to the mundane harmony of human beings, could "hold all Heav'n and Earth in happier union" (108). Cullen, on the other hand, completely ignores the progressive nature of Virgil's description. The difference between the *Eclogue* and the *Ode* has nothing to do with the validity of cyclical or linear conceptions of time. It has to do with the *order* in which the two poets describe the events leading up to the return of the golden age. Like Virgil, Milton insists that the birth of the miraculous child is only the beginning of a long and painful process that will not be completed until "the worlds last session" (163). Just as the second quest for the golden fleece and the second siege of Troy must precede the arrival of the golden age in *Eclogue IV,* so here the cessation of the oracles, the Crucifixion, and the Day of Judgement must all take place before "our bliss / Full and perfet is" (165-66). But by allowing us to glimpse, however briefly, the third and final act of the drama before the second act begins, Milton completely transforms the dynamics of the regenerative process. Experientially, the real climax of the *Nativity Ode* is not the appearance of the age of gold, as it is in the *Eclogue*, but the departure of the pagan deities.

As a result, Milton's *Ode* leaves an impression that has a good deal in common with the ending of another famous Nativity poem, T.S. Eliot's "Journey of the Magi." "Were we led all that way for Birth or Death?" asks the narrator:

> There was a Birth certainly,
> We had evidence and no doubt. I had seen birth and death,
> But had thought they were different; this Birth was
> Hard and bitter agony for us, like Death, our death. [35-39]

In just the same way, the *Nativity Ode* concludes on a note of calculated ambiguity, for, as William Empson has pointed out in a classic essay, the language of the final stanzas suggests nightfall as well as dawn, death as well as birth, loss as well as renewal:

> So when the Sun in bed,
> Curtain'd with cloudy red,
>   Pillows his chin upon an Orient wave,
> The flocking shadows pale,

Troop to th'infernal Jail,
   Each fetter'd Ghost slips to his several grave,
And the yellow-skirted Fayes,
Fly after the Night-steeds, leaving their Moon-lov'd maze.

But see the Virgin blest,
Hath laid her Babe to rest.
   Time is our tedious Song should here have ending;
Heav'ns youngest teemed star,
Hath fixed her polisht Car,
   Her sleeping Lord with Handmaid Lamp attending:
And all about the Courtly Stable,
Bright harnest Angels sit in order serviceable. [229-44]

We have been told in the opening lines that dawn is about to break, but, in Empson's words, the scene here "suggests nightfall; the ending of labour, and a lamp coming to guard a sleeper, now laid to rest."[47] What began as an *aubade* is ending as a lullaby. We know, too, that the poem's subject is birth, yet the phrase "Hath laid her babe to rest," coming as it does hard on the heels of the "grave" in line 234, inevitably suggests death as well as sleep.[48] A poem on "the morning of Christ's nativity" has become a poem on the mourning of Christ's nativity.

It is difficult, therefore, to understand how Balachandra Rajan can assert that the *Nativity Ode* "celebrates a happy event with a kind of crystalline joy."[49] T.K. Meier is surely much closer to the mark when he calls attention to "the joylessness of this formulation of the birth of Christ."[50] From the very beginning of the poem, I would suggest, the death of the old man has cast a shadow over the birth of the new. In William James's words, "the sense of our present wrongness is a far more distinct piece of our consciousness than is the imagination of any positive ideal that we can aim at. In a majority of cases, indeed, the sin almost exclusively engrosses the attention, so that conversion is a process of struggling away from sin rather than of striving towards righteousness."[51] Unregenerate Nature thus reacts to Christ's arrival not with the traditional expressions of joy that had characterized such poems as Dunbar's "Rorate caeli desuper" and Herrick's "Christmas

Caroll," but with fear and shame, seeking to hide her "foul defor-
mities" (44) with a modest veil of snow. Her lover, the sun, like-
wise seeks to hide his head "for shame" (80). The strong sense of
sin and unworthiness that had characterized the poet himself in
the Nativity poems of Donne, Herbert, Jonson, and Vaughan has
here been transferred to the natural world, "Pollute with sinful
blame" (41)—hence, perhaps, the absence of the traditional ox
and ass from Milton's stable.

What is more, the emphasis on the negative stage of the
conversion process affects even those sections of the narrative that
might be expected to be positive. It may not be surprising that the
advent of peace is described merely as an absence of war:

> *No* War or Battel's sound
> Was heard the world around:
>   The idle Spear and Shield were high up hung,
> The hooked Chariot stood
> *Un*stain'd with hostile blood,
>   The Trumpet spake *not* to the armed throng.
> [53-58, my emphasis]

Virgil, after all, had characterized the first stage of the world's
transformation as a series of negatives in the *Eclogue*—"untilled,"
"uncalled," "unasked." But it surely is surprising that the beatific
vision itself should consist largely in the absence of evil:

> For if such holy Song
> Enwrap our fancy long,
>   Time will run back, and fetch the age of gold,
> And speckl'd vanity
> Will sicken soon and die,
>   And leprous sin will melt from earthly mould
> And Hell it self will pass away,
> And leave her dolorous mansions to the peering day.
> [132-40]

In place of the new Jerusalem, Milton shows us an abandoned
leper-house.

The explanation for this pervasive negativity is to be found not so much in any failure of imagination on Milton's part as in his general conception of the human condition. As he explained later in his career in *De Doctrina Christiana*, the fruit of the tree of knowledge was so called "from the event." In the state of innocence the first pair experienced nothing but good. They could conceive of evil, it followed, only as an absence of the good they enjoyed; they knew evil *by* good. Thanks to the Fall, however, the moral status quo was reversed, with the result that in the postlapsarian world evil is the given and good can be conceived only as an absence of evil; we know good by evil, or, as Milton put it in *De Doctrina*, "since Adam tasted (the forbidden fruit) . . . we know good only by means of evil."[52] The strategy of exclusion dominates the *Nativity Ode* because in Milton's view it is the only way in which fallen human beings can begin to apprehend the paradisal state of perfection. In the postlapsarian world the light of heaven is "unsufferable" (8), the angelic song is "unexpressive" (116). As the heirs of Adam and Eve we can do no more than glimpse the coming age of gold, and then only as a privation of evil. In the meantime, trapped in the long-drawn-out "moment" of transition preceding the millennium, we must be content with the poetry of absence.

2

VIRTUE AND VIRGINITY

By these steps justice advances to the greatest height.
The first step of virtue is to abstain from evil works;
the second, to abstain also from evil words; the third,
to abstain even from the thoughts of evil things.
—Lactantius, *Divine Institutes*, 6.13

DURING THE COURSE OF SOME good-natured fun at the expense of critics who overinterpret *Comus*, Robert M. Adams offers a rebuttal of the notion that the magical herb the brothers receive from the Attendant Spirit to ward off Comus's enchantments might symbolize the operation of divine grace. "If haemony is grace," Adams objects, "there is a gross, immediate breach of tact in Thyrsis' declaration that in this country it is: 'Unknown, and like esteem'd, and the dull swayn Treads on it dayly with his clouted shoon' (634-35). An audience of country gentle folk would scarcely have been edified by this thought, particularly the clerical members of it."[1] The fact is, however, that an audience of country gentle folk may never have heard the thought expressed, for the lines in question were probably not included in the text of *Comus* performed at Ludlow Castle in 1634.[2]

Adams was led into this error by his belief that "whatever Milton had to say in *Comus*, he did not alter it radically in the course of composition; whatever main shape the masque had, it evidently had from the beginning."[3] Recent studies of the masque's textual history by such scholars as Cedric Brown, John Creaser, John Shawcross, G.W. Smith Jr., and S.E. Sprott have revealed that, on the contrary, *Comus* underwent a series of major modifications between its original conception in 1634 and its publication in 1637.[4] To a far greater degree than that of any other work of Milton's, the text of *Comus* is profoundly unstable, so much so, in fact, that it seems to have been in a constant state of flux from the time it was first written down to the day it first appeared in print. Between 1634 and 1637, one might say, the masque itself passed through a prolonged Miltonic moment, during the course of which it was fundamentally transformed.

Comus is extant in two manuscripts (the Trinity manuscript, in Milton's own handwriting, and the Bridgewater manuscript, in the hand of a professional scribe) and three printed editions (the anonymous edition of 1637 and the editions of Milton's shorter poems that appeared in 1645 and l673). The relationship between these texts has been exhaustively analyzed by the scholars listed above, but its main features can be summarized as follows. Within the Trinity manuscript there are four layers of intention: Milton's original draft and three separate revisions that can be distinguished from each other by such evidence as the quality of the pen, the color of the ink, and variations in handwriting, spelling, and orthography.[5] Following Sprott, I shall refer to the original text as Trinity 1, and to the three layers of revision as, in what is believed to be chronological order, Trinity 2, 3, and 4. The Bridgewater manuscript, probably a presentation copy of the text actually performed at Ludlow, is based either on Trinity 2 or, as Sprott suggests, on an intervening manuscript that has not survived. At all events, it contains several critical changes that do not appear in any other extant version of the masque, notably the omission of a long passage in the Lady's first speech (lines 195-225), the reassignment of lines 871-82 and 938-57, and the relocation of most of the Attendant Spirit's epilogue (lines 976-99) to the beginning of the opening scene. Between 1634 and 1637 Milton produced the revisions in Trinity 3, which became in turn the basis for the first printed edition of 1637. Like the Bridgewater manuscript, however, the 1637 edition also contains some variants that did not appear in the Trinity manuscript, specifically the addition of the Lady's defense of virginity and Comus's reaction to it (779-806). After further, relatively minor revisions in Trinity 4, Milton included the masque in the collected edition of his shorter poems published in 1645. Based on the 1637 edition, this version incorporates the revisions in Trinity 4. The last edition in Milton's lifetime, 1673, does not differ in any significant respect from 1645 and can, for the purposes of this discussion, be discounted.

Most of the substantive variants that Milton introduced into the masque during the course of its evolution from Trinity 1 to Trinity 4 are located in the temptation scene. As originally conceived, it consisted of only three speeches—Comus's opening exhortation, the Lady's rebuttal, and Comus's rejoinder, interrupted by the arrival of the brothers. Since the last of these speeches remained more or less constant throughout Milton's revisions, we may concentrate on the longer, first two speeches, which underwent several crucial modifications as Milton's conception of the scene became increasingly dramatic.

In its original form in Trinity 1, Comus's opening speech began with his declaration of his power to chain up the Lady's nerves (659-62), continued with his insistence on the joyful atmosphere of his palace (666-71), and then expanded to develop his attack on "lean and shallow Abstinence" (706-55), culminating in the invitation to drink his "cordial Julep" in order to refresh the Lady's exhausted spirits (672-78 and 687-90). The argument of the speech as a whole thus described a wide arc, from the initial attempt to reconcile his victim to her predicament to the more theoretical and eloquent defense of unbridled hedonism and then back to the immediate situation with the offer of the cup. The Lady's reply, on the other hand, gradually moved away from the actual circumstances in which she found herself to a generalized defense of moderation. Countering Comus's opening claim of being able to ensnare her body, she declared that he could not touch her mind (662-65), after which she reproached him for his deceit and spurned the proferred cup (690-705). Only then did she revert to the central section of his speech with her exposition of the "holy dictate of spare Temperance" (756-79).

The first set of revisions (Trinity 2) breaks up this formal pattern of assertion and denial by inserting the Lady's counter to Comus's initial claim immediately after it is made, locating the persuasion to drink the julep and the Lady's refusal immediately afterwards, and only then proceeding to Comus's more theoretical arguments and the Lady's refutation of them, the gap between the refusal of the the potion and Comus's praise of hedonism being supplied by the two extra lines referring to the well-governed appetite (704-5). The result of this drastic reorganization is twofold. First, the argument gradually expands from the particular to the general, that is, from the issue of the Lady's alleged bondage, with its contrast between body and mind, to the issue of the proferred cup, with its promise of ease and refreshment, to the abstract argument on the theme of nature's bounty and the proper response to it. Second, the temptation to partake of the cup, which was the focal point of the first version of the scene, is now only a preliminary to the debate about the natural economy.

In the Bridgewater manuscript the temptation scene took this general form, but with two significant alterations. Comus's application of his doctrine of pleasure to the Lady's virgin beauty (737-55) was omitted, as was the Lady's reference to faith, hope, and chastity in her earlier soliloquy (195-225). In Trinity 3, Milton laid the ground for Comus's sexual temptation of the Lady by inserting lines 679-86 on the subject of her "dainty limms," and buttressed the Lady's refusal by the addition of lines 697-700, with their reference to her tempter's "lickerish baits." Finally, in the 1637 edition the scene was further modified by reintroducing the reference to the Lady's virginity and giving the Lady for the first time an explicit reply to it, the long passage in praise of the "sage and serious doctrine of Virginity" (779-99). It was these changes in Trinity 3 and the printed edition that created perhaps the most intractable problem in the interpretation of *Comus*, the relationship of temperance to virginity.

The problem emerges most clearly during the temptation scene as it appears in the printed editions of 1637 and 1645. Comus argues that, since Nature pours forth her wealth in such overwhelming abundance, those who follow the Stoics and the Cynics in praising "the lean and sallow Abstinence" (709) are not only acting ungratefully, but are also courting ecological disaster. In order to prevent a vast and destructive surplus from building up, he concludes, we should all consume Nature's gifts without restraint:

Wherefore did Nature powre her bounties forth
With such a full and unwithdrawing hand,
Covering the earth with odours, fruits, and flocks,
Thronging the Seas with spawn innumerable,
But all to please, and sate the curious taste?
And set to work millions of spinning Worms,
That in their green shops weave the smooth-hair'd silk
To deck her Sons, and that no corner might
Be vacant of her plenty, in her own loyns
She hutch't th'all-worshipt ore, and precious gems
To store her children with; If all the world
Should in a pet of temperance feed on Pulse,
Drink the clear stream, and nothing wear but Frieze,
Th'all-giver would be unthank't, would be unprais'd,
Not half his riches known, and yet despis'd,
And we should serve him as a grudging master,
As a penurious niggard of his wealth,
And live like Natures bastards, not her sons,
Who would be quite surcharg'd with her own weight,
And strangl'd with her waste fertility. [710-29]

Comus offers, in other words, only two possible courses of action: on the one hand, unrestrained self-indulgence; on the other, total self-denial.

The main burden of the Lady's reply is that there is a third alternative: moderation, or, as she calls it, temperance. This response to Nature's bounty, which Comus has falsely equated with abstinence, is now shown to consist in consuming "but a moderate and beseeming share" of what Nature has to offer—as opposed to the "vast excess" enjoyed by "the few" in "lewdly pampered luxury." It is the "swinish gluttony" of the unjust, she points out, that causes just men to pine "with want." To remedy the situation, she proposes that the human race should share Nature's full blessings in "unsuperfluous eeven proportion" (768-76). Her point is much the same as Gloucester's in *King Lear*:

Let the superfluous and lust-dieted man,
That slaves your ordinance, that will not see

> Because he does not feel, feel your power quickly;
> So distribution should undo excess
> And each man have enough. [4.1.67-71]

The Lady thus refuses to accept Comus's parody of temperance as total abstinence, and insists that moderation is the key to achieving a healthy balance between production and consumption.

The terms of this debate derive, of course, from the Aristotelian conception of virtue as a mean between two opposing extremes, one of defect, one of excess:

> The nature of moral qualities is such that they are destroyed by defect and by excess. The same applies to self-control, courage, and the other virtues: the man who shuns and fears everything and never stands his ground becomes a coward, whereas a man who knows no fear at all and goes to meet every danger becomes reckless. Similarly, a man who revels in every pleasure and abstains from none becomes self-indulgent, while he who avoids every pleasure like a boor becomes what might be called insensitive. Thus we see that self-control and courage are destroyed by excess and by deficiency and are preserved by the mean.[6]

Virtue is thus primarily a matter of accurate calculation, for the mean is not necessarily the exact midpoint between the extremes of excess and defect. It is rather, Aristotle insists, a "median relative to us, . . . an amount neither too large nor too small, and this is neither one nor the same for everybody" (2.6.42). Thus, if ten pounds of food is too much for a person to eat and two is too little, this does not mean that the arithmetical median, six pounds, is the right amount of food for everybody. Depending on our individual needs, the mean might be only four pounds for one person, eight for another. As the Lady observes, the mean is determined by the laws of "proportion" (773); all that is required is that each person receive a "beseeming share" (769) of Nature's blessings.

So far so good. In all this the Lady is clearly and unequivocally in the right. The problems begin to arise when we try to reconcile this level-headed and thoroughly humane position with the Lady's response to the two concrete temptations with which she is faced: Comus's persuasions to drink of the cup and his subsequent attempt to seduce her. To begin with the former, we know that she is tired and thirsty by the evidence of her earlier speeches and those of her brothers. Indeed, the very reason she now finds herself in this predicament is that they had gone off to find her some much needed refreshment while she rested:

> My brothers when they saw me wearied out
> With this long way, resolving here to lodge
> Under the spreading favour of these Pines,
> Stept as they se'd to the next Thicket side
> To bring me Berries, or such cooling fruit
> As the kind hospitable Woods provide. [182-87]

So, when Comus suggests that she has been "tird all day without repast" (688), he is describing her situation quite accurately. Unlike Comus's earlier victims, whom the Attendant Spirit described in his opening speech, the Lady would be drinking not as a result of "fond intemperate thirst" (67) but out of genuine need. When her host offers her the cup of julep, therefore, it might seem quite reasonable for her to accept it, provided that, in accordance with the principle of moderation, she does not partake of it greedily or intemperately. We in the audience know, of course, that the cup is enchanted, but the Lady does not share our knowledge, and she is consequently hard pressed to find an argument for refusing Comus's offer. "None," she declares, "But such as are good men can give good things" (702-3).

The real trouble starts, however, when we try to reconcile the Lady's doctrine of temperance with her reaction to Comus's suggestion that she

> be not coy, and be not cosend
> With that same vaunted name Virginity,
> Beauty is natures coyn, must not be hoorded,

> But must be currant, and the good thereof
> Consists in mutual and partak'n bliss. [737-41]

As William Kerrigan has observed, the most effective alternative the Lady could offer to this proposition "would be chastity, widely believed in the Renaissance, especially among Protestants, to include marriage. As temperance is to abstinence, so Protestant chastity to virginity."[7] Without accepting the conclusion that she should be wholly promiscuous, then, the Lady could very well have replied that in sexual matters temperance consists in monogamous marriage, that though she hasn't the slightest intention of spending nature's coin indiscriminately, she doesn't intend to hoard it either. But in fact she says nothing of the kind. Instead we hear:

> To him that dares
> Arm his profane tongue with contemptuous words
> Against the Sun-clad power of Chastity;
> Fain would I something say, yet to what end?
> Thou hast nor Ear nor Soul to apprehend
> The sublime notion, and high mystery
> That must be utter'd to unfold the sage
> And serious doctrine of Virginity. [780-87]

Sexual abstinence, it now appears, is the only alternative to the promiscuous libertinism that Comus urges on her. To quote Kerrigan again, the Lady "accepts the name given to her by her tempter. Her chastity is virginity, transvalued from a defective extremity to a 'sublime notion and high mystery.'"[8] Against the principle of sensual indulgence represented by Comus stands the principle of virginity represented by the Lady.

The problem with this is only too obvious: how can we reconcile the "holy dictate of spare Temperance" (767), which the Lady advocates in the middle of her temptation scene, with the "sage / And serious doctrine of Virginity" (786-87), which she defends twenty lines later. It would be hard to improve on A.E. Barker's account of the difficulty:

Comus strives to overcome her resolution by representing her virtue as an absurd and unlovely extreme. He ridicules the inflexible abstinence which uncompromisingly rejects nature's gifts, and cites the Lady's virginity—with its repudiation of the powers of youth and beauty—as a prime example of this represssive doctrine. In answer to the first part of this attack the Lady develops, with considerable effect, the doctrine of the mean. The extremes of undisciplined indulgence and of rigid abstinence are alike reprehensible; true virtue begins with temperance—the moderate and proportioned use of nature according to reason. But to the second part of the attack she replies with a categorical and cryptic assertion of "the sun-clad power of chastity" and an obscure reference to "the sage and serious doctrine of virginity." What distinction is to be made between these virtues and how they are to be related to temperance she deigns to tell neither Comus—who would perhaps not have understood but is easily convinced—nor us. And she does not indicate, as in the case of abstinence she has clearly indicated, at what point Comus's estimate of virginity is in error. We are left with the uncomfortable feeling that his interpretation of it as a perverse repudiation of powers with which nature has endued the Lady remains unrefuted.[9]

At one moment virtue is being defined as moderation, the mean between the extremes of excessive indulgence and total abstinence; at the next, it is being defined *as* a form of total abstinence. At one moment we are in the monistic world of Aristotle's *Ethics,* in which physical pleasures are harmless provided that we enjoy them in due measure; at the next, we are in the dualistic world of Plato's *Phaedo,* in which the lover of wisdom "will be set free as far as possible from the eye and the ear and, in short, from the whole body, because intercourse with the body troubles the soul, and hinders her from gaining truth and wisdom."[10]

Curiously enough, this fundamental contradiction has remained largely unexamined during the fifty-five years or so that have passed since the publication of Barker's analysis. To take just one example, in the most recent book-length study of the masque Cedric Brown remarks that the Lady's defense of virginity "creates a problem of accommodation" with her brother's speech on the same subject in the previous scene, but never mentions the still more serious problem of accommodation it creates with the Lady's exposition of temperance just a few lines earlier. All that remains of the difficulty that Barker identified is a casual oxymoron: "the drift of the debate [between Comus and the Lady]," Brown observes, "is easy to see. It is the maintenance of *chaste temperance* in the face of devilish persuasions to luxury."[11]

The reason that the incompatibility between temperance and virginity has attracted so little attention, I suspect, is that one of the two conflicting values has been virtually erased from Milton's text. For with the notable exception of William Kerrigan and Christopher Kendrick, who interpret the Lady's "reduction of chastity to virginity" in essentially Freudian terms, modern critics of the masque have gone to quite extraordinary lengths to evade or deny the fact that in its printed form *Comus* idealizes sexual abstinence.[12] The most popular tactic, which seems to have originated with A.S.P. Woodhouse, is to insist on "the separability of virginity and chastity" while at the same time claiming that "the central issue in *Comus* is not virginity, but chastity."[13] According to John Shawcross, for instance, "chastity, by which is meant purity in conduct and intention, is not the same as virginity (with its implications of celibacy and the rewards of Revelation 14:4), and the Lady's added lines differentiate the two. . . . In question, of course, is not virginity but a general doctrine of chastity. . . . Though a virgin, the real test is her chastity."[14] But though this distinction was certainly available to Milton—he would have encountered it in "our sage and serious poet" Spenser's *Faerie Queene*, among other places— in *Comus* the two terms are used interchangeably. As Shawcross notes elsewhere, "there seems to be a confounding of chastity and virginity" in the Elder Brother's parallel references to "true virginity" and the "arms of chastity" (436–40), as well as in the Attendant Spirit's plea that Sabrina help "a true virgin" and the latter's desire "To help ensnared chastity" (905–9).[15] But the same could surely be said of the Lady's defiant reply to her tempter, in which

"the Sun-clad power of Chastity" that Comus has derided and
"the sage / And serious doctrine of Virginity" that she would teach
him if only he were capable of understanding it are both logically
and grammatically identical.[16]

A second tactic is to purge virginity of its negative implica-
tions by treating it as an allegorical emblem for something more
positive. Thus, Georgia Christopher finds in it "a fitting symbol
for Reformation faith," and transforms the entire masque into a
theological contest between "*virginitas fidei*" or "doctrinal virgin-
ity," represented by the Lady, and "hermetic egoism," represented
by Comus.[17] Maryann McGuire, on the other hand, defines vir-
ginity as "an unswerving love of God expressed in all life's ac-
tions." The substitution of chastity for charity in the Lady's open-
ing speech, she argues, demonstrates that "chastity is Milton's ver-
sion of charity." In his treatment of chastity as an ideal of conduct,
therefore, Milton was concerned "not with human love, sexual
ethics, or the rituals of courtship, but with the Christian believer's
love for God and the effect of that love on his moral life."[18]

Quite apart from their inherent implausibility, these theolo-
gizing readings do rather less than justice to the quite explicit eroti-
cism of Comus's advances, with their references to the Lady's
"vermeil-tinctur'd lip," "love-darting eyes," and "tresses like the
morn" (752-53), not to mention his leering reference to her "dainty
limms" (680). But perhaps the most overtly sexual passage in the
masque is spoken not by Comus but by the Elder Brother in his
graphic account of the "lewd and lavish act of sin":

> when lust
> By unchaste looks, loose gestures, and foul talk,
> But most by lewd and lavish act of sin,
> Lets in defilement to the inward parts,
> The soul grows clotted by contagion,
> Imbodies and imbrutes, till she quite lose
> The divine property of her first being. [463-69]

One could hardly want a more specific rejection of carnal rela-
tions. Kerrigan believes that in these lines "the Elder Brother rep-
resents the sin of unchastity by eating and drinking," but the domi-

nant metaphor here is surely that of sexual congress.[19] As in Plato's description of the spirit's imprisonment in matter in the *Phaedo*, which the Elder Brother had evidently been reading, the male organ is the instrument not of generation but of "defilement" that contaminates the woman's "inward parts" with the "contagion" of physical lust. The act of procreation has been transformed into a species of moral and spiritual infection.[20]

Nor do the less obvious references to human sexuality in the masque present it any more favorably. For whether or not Barbara Breasted and Leah Marcus are right in detecting a connection between the Lady's dilemma and the fates of the Countess of Castlehaven, Elizabeth Audley, and Margery Evans, there is no denying the fact that the text of *Comus* is saturated with references to virgins who have been either raped or dehumanized, or both, as a result of their male admirers' passion.[21] Philomena (566-67), who was raped by Tereus and transformed into a nightingale, Medusa (447-52), who was raped by Neptune and turned into a snaky-headed monster, Callisto (421-27), who was raped by Jove and changed into a bear, Echo (230), who was pursued by Pan and torn into pieces by a band of shepherds, Daphne (659-62), who was pursued by Apollo and transformed by her father into a laurel tree, and Syrinx (345), who was pursued by Pan and turned into a reed by her sisters, all testify to the destructive consequences of male erotic desire. Only Psyche, "far above in spangled sheen" (1002), enjoys the fruits of marriage. It would be difficult, surely, to think of a work that presents sexuality in a more negative light. In the world of *Comus*, terrestrial Cupid is a beast of prey. Small wonder if virginity is the supreme virtue.

In view of the critical trends I have just described, it is hardly surprising that the only sustained attempt to analyze the relationship between virginity and temperance took place over forty years ago. In 1951, a decade after Barker's study originally appeared, E.M.W. Tillyard published a famous essay entitled "The Action of Comus," in which he undertook to defend the masque against the charge of philosophical inconsistency by examining its textual history. According to Tillyard, the modifications Milton introduced into the 1637 printed version of *Comus* effectively resolved what in the earlier version of the masque was an unresolved dispute, modeled on an academic disputation, between abstinence, defended by the Lady, and indulgence, advocated by Comus. The additional lines (1000-1011) that Milton added to the spirit's epilogue in Trinity 3, with their reference to the garden of Adonis, and thus to the third book of Spenser's *Faerie Queene*, implied a vision of monogamous marriage and generative human love that reconciled the claims of chastity and sexual pleasure: "The play concerns chastity and the Lady is the heroine. Comus advocates incontinence, Acrasia, . . . the Lady advocates abstinence. The Attendant Spirit gives the solution, advocating the Aristotelian middle course, which for the Lady is the right one; and it is marriage."[22] This, Michael Macklem suggested in a later article based on Tillyard's, signaled a shift in Milton's value system from an other-worldly ideal of asceticism (represented by virginity) to a this-worldly ideal of moderation (represented by chaste marriage).[23]

It seems to me that both critics got this argument exactly back to front, and that they did so because they failed to take into account the textual evidence in its entirety. What Tillyard and Macklem did, in effect, was simply to ignore the Bridgewater, or performed, version of the masque altogether and to lump all the strata of the Trinity manuscript into one single version of the masque, which they referred to collectively as the "early" or "first" version.[24] Thus, Tillyard states early in his article that the Bridgewater manuscript, "containing a slightly altered and abbreviated version for stage production, need not concern us. The various changes within the Trinity manuscript have no decisive importance; and the significant changes are those between the completed first draft as contained in the Trinity manuscript (which I call the first or 1634 version) and the first printed text (which I call the 1637 version)."[25] The foregoing survey of the masque's textual history reveals that he was completely mistaken, both about the slightness of the alterations embodied in the Bridgewater manuscript and about the unimportance of the changes in the various levels of revision in the Trinity manuscript. Likewise, Macklem dismissed the Bridgewater manuscript in a footnote—the Bridgewater manuscript, he stated, "the one actually used for the production, shows certain omissions and alterations made for technical theatrical reasons"—and asserted, quite wrongly, that "ex-

amination of the Trinity MS. (containing the complete text as
Milton wrote it for performance in 1634) and the text of the printed
edition of 1637 reveals that the doctrine of virginity was stated in
the first draft, and the doctrine of temperance in the second."[26]
If both critics had examined the Bridgewater manuscript more
closely, however, they would have discovered that the performed
version of the masque—that is, the 1634 text as it was actually
staged at Ludlow—far from defending virginity, hardly mentions
it at all. The only references to it that the Ludlow audience heard
were contained in the Elder Brother's speech on the efficacy of
sexual purity and in the Attendant Spirit's invocation of Sabrina.
The Lady's famous vision of Faith, Hope, and Chastity (lines 195-
225) and Comus's attempt at persuading her to spend nature's coin
indiscriminately (lines 737-55) were omitted from the acting ver-
sion, while Comus's allusion to the Lady's dainty limbs (679-87)
and her steadfast defense of sexual abstinence (779-806) were added
later. The theme of the 1634 text presented to the Earl of
Bridgewater and his family, then, was quite straightforward: It was
temperance pure and simple. As Balachandra Rajan has put it,
Milton now "had a straightforward disputation between Comus
and the Lady restricted to temperance and the right use of na-
ture."[27] The Attendant Spirit announces in his opening speech
that those who drink of Comus's cup are victims of "fond intem-
perate thirst" (67), Comus derides the notion that all the world
"should in a pet of temperance feed on Pulse" (720), and the Lady
retorts by defending "the holy dictate of spare Temperance" (767).
What is more, the ideal of temperance is implicit both in the
younger brother's praise of divine philosophy as "a perpetual feast
of nectar'd sweets, / Where no crude surfet raigns" (478-79) and
in the Lady's criticism of the peasants' "Riot, and ill manag'd
Merriment" (172-79). Most important of all, the Lady wins her
victory over "sensual Folly, and Intemperance" (975) merely by
refusing to drink from a cup symbolizing intemperance. Her vir-
ginity has never been implicitly or explicitly threatened, and the
philosophical contradiction between abstinence and temperance
that Barker pointed out is completely absent.[28]
    The masque of temperance became the masque of virginity
only in the 1637 printed text, in which Milton restored the lines

omitted for the Ludlow performance and added another thirty-five or so on the same subject. Far from moving from a defense of virginity to a defense of temperance, as Macklem claimed, the masque moves in precisely the opposite direction. It is in the printed text of 1637, not the performed text of 1634, that virginity emerges as the central issue in the temptation scene. Neither side of the unresolved dispute between abstinence and promiscuity that Tillyard sought to resolve with the doctrine of the mean was represented in the Ludlow performance. Indeed, if Milton had wanted to extoll the "virtues of the Aristotelian middle course," as Tillyard believed, all he had to do was print the text as it stood in the Bridgewater manuscript. Why, then, did he not only reintroduce, but also reinforce, the fundamentally incompatible theme of virginity? How are we to account for the presence of two radically contradictory definitions of virtue in the published version of the masque?

One possible answer, I believe, is to be found in a basic contradiction that was built into the Renaissance worldview itself. For the "great chain of being," with its familiar hierarchy of orders and degrees, was not only an ontological system; with the Deity at the top and the Devil at the bottom, it was also a moral one.[29] As a result, it was possible to extrapolate two quite different ethical imperatives from the natural order. On the one hand, you could argue that, since God had created a hierarchical structure in the first place, it was the duty of every creature to keep its divinely appointed station, to preserve the status quo. Thus, when Dante enquires in the *Divine Comedy* whether Piccarda and her fellow spirits in the sphere of the moon aspire to a more exalted position in the heavenly scheme of things, she explains that she and her companions are perfectly content to remain where they are, because "If we could wish to bide in loftier bowers, / Our wish would jangle with that will of His / Which hath assigned our proper place and powers."[30] By the same token, mere mortals would be defying the will of God if they attempted to join the celestial ranks while they were still living on this earth. Poised between the angels above them, with whom they shared the gift of reason, and the animals below them, with whom they shared their bodily appetites, the descendants of Adam and Eve should neither give themselves over completely to their bestial desires nor devote themselves exclusively to their rational powers. As Ottaviano pointed out in *The Book of the Courtier,* "it is not well to extirpate the passions altogether, . . . [for] when moderated by temperance they are an aid to virtue . . . if they were wholly taken away, [they] would leave the reason weak and languid, so that it could effect little."[31] The proper course, rather, was to maintain an appropriate balance between reason and appetite by using the former to control and moderate the latter—the doctrine of temperance.

On the other hand, you could argue equally plausibly that, since the great chain of being was also a hierarchy of excellence, the higher up the chain you could ascend the better. According to this polarized view of reality, we inhabit not an undivided universe of good, in which all pleasures are permissible provided they are enjoyed in moderation, but a dualistic universe of good and evil, in which those pleasures associated with our lower, animal nature are intrinsically corrupt. If this were the case, it was clearly the duty of human beings to deny and if possible to eradicate their animal appetites altogether in order to cultivate their angelic reason—the doctrine of abstinence.

The tension between these two ethical systems and the assumptions underlying them is evident everywhere in the literature of the Renaissance, from More's *Utopia,* where the "holier" priests "utterly reject the pleasures of this life as harmful, eagerly and earnestly striving for the joys of the life to come," while the "wiser" priests "avoid no pleasure so long as it does not interfere with their labour,"[32] to Donne's *The Extasie,* where the lovers whose souls have achieved a transcendent union outside their physical bodies finally recognize that they must "descend / T'affections and to faculties, / Which sense may reach and apprehend" (65-67). Over and over again, the Aristotelian acceptance of the material world and its pleasures collides with the Platonic impulse to abandon the realm of the senses in pursuit of pure spirituality.[33]

In *Paradise Lost* Milton more or less successfully resolves this conflict by making the former, with its emphasis on preserving the status quo, the necessary prelude to the latter, with its emphasis on ascending the natural order. Adam learns from Raphael that:

> time may come when men
> With Angels may participate, and find
> No inconvenient Diet, nor too light Fare:
> And from these corporal nutriments perhaps
> Your bodies may at last turn all to Spirit,
> Improv'd by tract of time, and wingd ascend
> Ethereal, as wee. [5.493-99]

There is, however, a condition. Before they undertake the Platonic ascent, Adam and Eve must first "be found obedient, and retain / Unalterably firm his love entire / Whose progenie you are" (5.501-3). And what this turns out to mean in practice is that the first pair must faithfully observe the Aristotelian rule of temperance in their material garden. Surrounded by a superabundance of physical and intellectual pleasures, they must learn to control their appetites, not to suppress them altogether. Indeed, Milton explicitly denounces the kind of self-denial exemplified by More's "holier" priests:

> Whatever Hypocrites austerely talk
> Of puritie and place and innocence,
> Defaming as impure what God declares
> Pure, and commands to som, leaves free to all.
> Our Maker bids increase, who bids abstain
> But our destroyer, foe to God and Man? [4.744-49]

The original human condition, in short, is conceived as a quintessentially Miltonic moment of transition between non-entity on the one hand and spiritual transcendence on the other. Only when this "decisive instant" (to borrow Ruskin's phrase again) of temperate indulgence in the pleasures of the flesh is complete will Adam and Eve be permitted to join the angels in their ethereal condition. Having enjoyed the goods of the material world in moderation, they will eventually achieve the goal of those who renounce it: they will become pure spirit.

What makes this extraordinary combination of this-worldly and other-worldly value systems possible, of course, is the fact that the Fall has not yet taken place and that, as a result, physical nature is still wholly innocent. The moral polarization of the universe implicit in the ethic of abstinence has not yet occurred, so Adam and Eve's prospective transformation "all to spirit" is not so much a flight from corruption as it is a progression from a lesser to a greater good, a sublimation rather than a rejection of their bodily appetites. All Milton's other poems, however, are set in the postlapsarian world in which good is associated exclusively with the upper, spiritual levels of reality, evil exclusively with the lower, material ones. From the very outset of their moral experience, therefore, the virtuous will "scorn the sordid world and unto heaven aspire."[34] No longer is there any preliminary period of temperate enjoyment. Trapped in this "darksome house of mortal clay,"[35] we are morally obliged to do everything we can to hasten the day when "our heav'nly guided soul shall climb / Then all this Earthy grossness quit."[36]

In *Comus* Milton thus posits a universe that is radically dualistic.[37] Above is the spiritual realm of grace, "where those immortal shapes / Of bright aerial Spirits live insphear'd / In Regions milde of calm and serene Air" (2-4). Below is the material realm of "this dim spot, / Which men call Earth," where fallen humanity strives "to keep up a frail and Feaverish being" among the "rank vapors of this Sin-worn mould" (5-17). In such a universe the path to virtue clearly lies upward; those who seek salvation will do so not by tempering their animal appetites like Adam and Eve in the garden of Eden, but by attempting to deny them—by practicing the doctrine of abstinence. As the Elder Brother puts it:

So dear to Heav'n is Saintly chastity,
That when a soul is found sincerely so,
A thousand liveried Angels lacky her,

. . . .
Till oft converse with heav'nly habitants
Begin to cast a beam on th'outward shape,
The unpolluted temple of the mind,
And turns it by degrees to the souls essence,
Till all be made immortal. [453-63][38]

As a result, critics of the masque often write as if the only alternative to this ascent into the world of pure spirit were the degrading metamorphosis undergone by those who partake of Comus's "baneful cup" (525),

> whose pleasing poison
> The visage quite transforms of him that drinks,
> And the inglorious likeness of a beast
> Fixes instead, unmoulding reasons mintage
> Character'd in the face. [526-30]

John Reesing, for instance, argues that *Comus* dramatizes two opposing kinds of transformation, "into a beast, or into a god," while Balachandra Rajan believes that "the masque reflects man's central position on the Great Chain of Being, confronted with the way up into being or the way down into self-annihilation."[39] Yet the fact is that the Lady's exposition of nature's "sober laws" (766) implicitly recognizes a third option, the possibility of remaining in the "central position" by preserving a stable balance between the divine and the bestial components in human nature. So powerful was the influence of the alternative interpretation of the natural hierarchy that, even within an essentially Platonic framework, Milton still found room for the Aristotelian doctrine of temperance, with its insistence on the essential goodness of "most innocent nature" (762).[40] The "drear" (37) and "hideous" (520) wood, whose "blind mazes" (181) and "perplex't paths" (37) clearly symbolize the darkness and confusion of the fallen world, is simultaneously a "kind" and "hospitable" (187) refuge, whose "prosperous growth" (270) offers "cooling fruit" (186) to the exhausted traveler. Dante's *selva oscura* coexists with Shakespeare's forest of Arden.

In this connection it is important to remember that the Lady does not attempt to refute Comus's eloquent account of Nature's benevolent vitality. Indeed, her explication of "the holy dictate of spare Temperance" (767) is grounded on the very same premise as her tempter's argument, that the "blessings" (772) of the physical world are essentially good. What she objects to is Comus's fallacious conclusion that Nature's children "should be riotous / With her abundance" (763-64). A "well-govern'd and wise appetite"

(705), she insists, will reject both the "lean and sallow Abstinence" (709) Comus falsely attributes to her and the "vast excess" (771) he himself advocates. Not for a moment does she endorse the Attendant Spirit's *contemptus mundi*.

Even in its original form, then, the masque contained an implicit contradiction between the this-worldly ethic it celebrated and the other-worldly structure it depicted. The growing prominence of virginity in Milton's revisions merely brings his morality into closer and closer agreement with his metaphysics. Given the pervasive dualism of his early works, it was almost inevitable that abstinence rather than temperance would eventually emerge as the dominant ethical imperative in his first extended treatment of moral experience.

The shift from temperance to chastity, both in the evolution of the text of the masque and in the Lady's response to her tempter, may also reflect a deep-seated tension within the concept of temperance itself. As we have seen, the doctrine of the mean attempts to locate virtue along an essentially quantitative axis, at one end of which lies defect and at the other excess. The ideal of moderation is essentially a matter of accurate calculation. Seen from a qualitative point of view, however, virtue is itself a moral extreme, opposed to the twin vices of defect and excess. In Aristotle's words, "in respect of its essence and the definition of its essential nature virtue is a mean, but in regard to goodness and excellence it is an extreme" (2.7.44). Faced with a choice between good and evil, a moral person would obviously be mistaken to seek out an intermediate position in accordance with the doctrine of the mean. And indeed no one was more aware of this than Milton himself. The doctrine of the mean, he declared in *Of Reformation*, "is a fallacious rule, unless understood only of the actions of virtue about things indifferent; for if it be found that those two extremes be vice and virtue, falsehood and truth, the greater extremity of virtue and superlative truth we run into, the more virtuous, the more wise we become."[41]

Drama, and especially drama with its roots in the English tradition of the morality play, tends to deal precisely in such polarities. To a greater extent than any other literary form, perhaps, it operates in terms of truth and falsehood, right and wrong, salvation and damnation—antitheses between which the middle way can only be a pallid form of accommodation. The task of characters like Everyman, Mankind, and their Renaissance successors is not to navigate between the personified vices and virtues that flank them but to choose the right side. By its very nature, drama invites us to apprehend human experience in qualitative rather than quantitative terms, and as a result moderation is one of the least dramatic of the virtues. Indeed, in practice it can often look dangerously like the policy of moral compromise—just as the policy of compromise can all too easily be misrepresented as the practice of moderation. "I observe," wrote Milton in *An Apology Against a Pamphlet*, "that fear and dull disposition, lukewarmness and sloth, are not seldomer wont to clothe themselves under the affected name of moderation than true and lively zeal is customably disparaged with the term of indiscretion, bitterness, and choler."[42] When good faces evil or truth confronts falsehood, the middle of the road is neither the best nor the safest place to be.

What is more, as Aristotle originally noted, the mean is only rarely equidistant from the extremes that frame it: "In some cases it is the deficiency and in others the excess that is more opposed to the median. For example, . . . in the case of self-control it is not the defect, insensitivity, but the excess, self-indulgence, which is more opposite" (2.9.48). The reason for this, he went on to argue, has to do with a basic characteristic of human nature, that "the more we are naturally attracted to anything, the more opposed to the median does this thing appear to be. For example, since we are naturally more attracted to pleasure we incline more easily to self-indulgence than to a disciplined kind of life. We describe as more opposed to the mean those things toward which our tendency is stronger; and for that reason the excess, self-indulgence, is more opposed to self-control than is its corresponding deficiency" (2.9.48). This tendency to transform the tripartite structure of the theory of the mean into a simple binary opposition has a consequence that Aristotle did not note, however. For since the mean allies itself with the extreme closest to it against the extreme farthest from it, the mean inevitably takes on something of the character of its extremist ally. Self-control becomes increasingly difficult to distinguish from insensitivity as they make common cause against self-indulgence. Indeed, Milton argued in *The Doctrine and Discipline of Divorce* and in *Colasterion* that the most effective way of combating any particular extreme was to enlist the support of its polar opposite. In rejecting the Pharisees' attitude toward divorce, for example, Christ behaved "like a wise Physician, administring one excesse against another to reduce us to a perfect mean: Where the Pharises were strict, there Christ seems remisse; where they were too remisse, he saw it needful to seem most severe: . . . as when we bow things the contrary way, to make them come to their naturall straitnesse."[43] If this is the tactic that the Lady is employing in *Comus*, then her invocation of virginity in response to Comus's advocacy of promiscuity might simply be a deliberate exaggeration designed to draw her opponent towards the mean.

At all events, this kind of alliance between the mean and the extreme that most resembles it is reinforced, Aristotle pointed out, by their adversary's habit of lumping them together. "People at the extremes," he wrote, "each push the man in the middle over to the other extreme: a coward calls a brave man reckless and a reckless man calls a brave man a coward, and similarly with the other qualities" (2.8.48). And in just the same way, of course, a self-indulgent character is likely to call a self-controlled man insensitive—hence Comus's equation of temperance with abstinence.

The natural conclusion of Aristotle's analysis is that "the first concern of a man who aims at the median should be to avoid the extreme which is more opposed to it" (2.9.50). A writer who wishes to portray the virtue of fortitude is likely, therefore, to put all the emphasis on the threat posed by cowardice rather than recklessness, and a writer whose theme is the virtue of moderation will almost certainly identify its major antagonist as over-indulgence rather than insensitivity. As a result, characters like Spenser's Sir Guyon and Milton's Lady, who represent the virtue of temperance, find themselves tempted from only one direction, the extreme of excess. No one in the *Faerie Queene* tries to persuade Sir Guyon to reject the pleasures of the world in order to become a hermit, for instance, and no one in *Comus* attempts to convince the Lady of the desirability of becoming a nun. Attacked on one flank only, the exemplars and defenders of the *via media* are thus driven further and further toward the opposite extreme of defect. So though Sir Guyon approves of Medina in theory, under the pressure of resisting those temptations embodied exclusively by Perissa, he moves inexorably toward the opposite extreme of Elissa in his encounters with Mammon, Phaedria, and Acrasia. We can see the process taking place particularly clearly, I think, in Milton's retrospective interpretation of Sir Guyon's temptation in *Areopagitica*, where the patron of temperance is exposed to the bower of earthly bliss so that "he might see and know, *and yet abstain*."[44] In much the same way, the internal dynamics of the temptation scene in *Comus* virtually guarantee that the defender of temperance will abandon the middle ground and turn into a militant defender of abstinence.

What is more, the pressure to move away from the mean toward one of the extremes may have been reinforced in Milton's mind, if not in the Lady's, by a second factor. For the Aristotelian concept of temperance as a *via media* between deficiency and excess is the structural equivalent of the "decisive instant" that intervenes between two opposing narrative sequences in Giotto's paintings and Milton's poems. The important point here is that in both cases the "betweenness" of the intermediate position renders it radically unstable. As we have seen, the Miltonic moment is almost by definition transitional; it looks forward to an imminent revolution. In much the same way, one might argue, the Aristotelian mean provides only a temporary state of equilibrium; sooner or later it will be driven to align itself with whichever extreme it finds more compatible. However inconsistent the coexistence of temperance and virginity in the Lady's speech might appear to be from a strictly logical point of view, psychologically the move from the one to the other is entirely plausible.

Virginity, I want to suggest in conclusion, may also play a major role in Milton's treatment of the other crucial issue that confronted him in *Comus*: to what extent are human beings capable of acting virtuously without divine assistance? In terms of my initial discussion, to what extent is the transition that takes place during the Miltonic moment dependent upon external forces? At the "decisive instant" of her life, how free is the Lady to determine the outcome of her trial? Milton addresses this issue most explicitly in the final six lines of the masque where, in John Diekhoff's words, the Attendant Spirit "states the simple moral":[45]

> Mortals that would follow me,
> Love vertue, she alone is free,
> She can teach ye how to clime
> Higher than the spheary chime;
> Or if vertue feeble were,
> Heav'n it self would stoop to her. [l018-23]

Unfortunately, Professor Diekhoff does not tell us what the "simple moral" of this passage is, and, still more unfortunately, those critics who have attempted to do so offer totally contradictory versions of it. About the first four lines there is no particular difficulty; virtue, the Attendant Spirit announces, can instruct human beings how to ascend to heaven. The problem arises when we come to the final couplet. Does "Or" introduce a genuine alternative or is Milton using the word to mean "otherwise"—it can't be raining or he would have opened his umbrella? And how are we to interpret the conditional clause that follows? Does it imply that virtue is or is not feeble? Robert M. Adams prefers the second alternative. "The last word of line 1022, 'were,' is crucial here," he writes. "To parse its grammar out, it is a third person singular subjunctive form used in a subordinate clause to indicate a condition contrary to fact." By writing the last couplet in this form "Milton can only have intended to convey that if virtue were feeble (which he did not think she was and had not represented her as being), heaven would stoop like a falcon to help her."[46] Cleanth Brooks and John Hardy, on the contrary, opt for the first alternative. By the time we reach the epilogue, they claim, Milton has made it unambiguously clear that virtue is not self-sufficient: "That heaven does stoop and that such assistance is absolutely essential, the entire poem has already demonstrated."[47] And George Whiting, somewhat confusingly, seems to hold both views at once: "If virtue feeble were—but virtue is not feeble—heaven itself would stoop to her. Heaven does stoop; God watches over his own."[48] Why heaven "does stoop" even though "virtue is not feeble" he nowhere deigns to explain.

The disagreement is important not only because the final lines of a masque traditionally encapsulate its moral (A.E. Dyson's description of the epilogue as a moment of "exquisite lyrical relief" hardly does justice to its traditional didactic function),[49] but also because in this particular case the two rival interpretations imply two diametrically opposed evaluations of the efficacy of virtue and consequently two diametrically opposed descriptions of the human predicament. If Adams is right, *Comus* is a ringing affirmation of the humanist confidence in the capacity of morally enlightened human beings to act virtuously on their own initiative. If Brooks and Hardy are right, *Comus* reaffirms the Puritan belief that we cannot act virtuously without the assistance of divine grace. And if Whiting is right, the masque is simply an incoherent theological muddle.

The problem is further complicated by the different ways in which Milton uses the word "virtue" in the same passage. In line 1019 virtue is clearly a personified abstraction, the same celestial being who in the Attendant Spirit's opening speech awards a crown "to her true servants" (10). As such she belongs in the same ontological category as Milton's other favorite personifications, Truth, Justice, Peace, and Mercy, the four daughters of God. But in line 1022 virtue seems to be particular rather than general, internal rather than external, a property of one of her servants rather than a personification of the ideal to which they aspire. If a virtuous person lacks the strength to make the ascent described in the previous lines, the Attendant Spirit seems to be saying, then heaven will descend to aid her. At one moment virtue is a celestial abstraction, at the next a frail human being in need of help. The difficulty can be resolved, perhaps, by assuming that "feeble" refers not to virtue's inability to ascend higher than the "spheary chime" but to her inability to teach mortals how to do so—if virtue's instruction is not sufficiently persuasive, heaven would descend to reinforce it—but there is no denying that on at least one other occasion in the masque Milton uses "virtue" to mean a virtuous person. "Vertue may be assail'd," declares the Elder Brother of the Lady's plight, "but never hurt, / Surpriz'd by unjust force, but not enthrall'd" (589-90; cf. 373-74).

The uncertainty concerning virtue's status in the Attendant

Spirit's epilogue reinforces our doubts about the grammar of the final two lines. For if virtue is a personification, an abstract quality that has been given human form, then she is an idea to which the descendents of Adam and Eve may aspire but which they do not necessarily attain. But if virtue is an exemplification, a real person whose behavior demonstrates the abstract quality in practice, then it may be possible for individual men and women to achieve goodness in their earthly lives. Once again we are brought face-to-face with the question that lies at the heart of *Comus:* are fallen human beings capable of acting virtuously without supernatural assistance?

The same question is posed, incidentally, by the only other overt reference in the masque to the issue of human self-sufficiency, the Elder Brother's reminder that the Lady has a hidden strength, "Which, if Heav'n gave it, may be term'd her own" (419). But what if heaven did not give it? Would her hidden strength then not belong to her? The problem here obviously has to do with the apparent breakdown in logic: we would normally assume that if the Lady's hidden strength is a gift it does not belong to her, and that if it is not a gift it does. We would therefore expect the Elder Brother to say either "which, if heaven did not give it, may be termed her own" or "which, if heaven gave it, may not be termed her own." In fact, he seems to assert in one breath two mutually exclusive propositions: that the Lady's strength is a gift, and that it is the Lady's own. The only solution is to assume that Milton is using "if" not in the conditional sense at all but in the concessive—that he means not "the lady's hidden strength may be termed her own on condition that heaven gave it," but rather "even if heaven gave her this hidden strength it may still, for all practical purposes, be called her own." In either case, to reverse Touchstone's aphorism, there seems to be much "if" in virtue.

These ambiguities and uncertainties, I want to suggest, are the grammatical correlative of the fundamental ideological contradiction that the masque attempts to resolve: the conflict between the Puritan insistence on the indispensable role of divine grace and the humanist confidence in the efficacy of individual human effort. As a student at one of the finest humanist educational institutions in seventeenth-century England (St. Paul's School), and at the intellectual headquarters of the Puritan movement (Cambridge University), Milton could hardly have avoided being thoroughly exposed to both beliefs, and *Comus* is only the first in a lifelong series of efforts he made to negotiate between them.

With its emphasis on the crucial role of reason in the conduct of a virtuous life, the humanist position naturally regarded a sound education as an essential ingredient in the development of a morally autonomous individual. Indeed, as Paul O. Kristeller has pointed out, the humanist movement was in essence an educational program designed to produce morally informed men and women.[50] Believing as they did that "if good and evil were well recognized and understood, no one would fail to prefer good and eschew evil," the humanists of the sixteenth and seventeenth centuries sought to promote public and private virtue by instructing their contemporaries in literature, history, and philosophy, but above all in ethics.[51] Knowledge was the key to virtue, and knowledge was the product of education. A *humanista*, therefore, was first and foremost a teacher, and the principal humanist institution was the school. All these assumptions are clearly evident in Milton's own tract on education. "The end then of learning," he declared, "is to repair the ruins of our first parents by regaining to know God aright . . . as we may the nearest by possessing our souls of true virtue, which being united to the heavenly grace of faith makes up the highest perfection."[52] Only at the very last moment is the humanist confidence in the redemptive capacity of the knowledge conferred by education supplemented by the Puritan insistence on the saving power of faith conferred by grace. Indeed, the "heavenly grace of faith" sounds almost like an afterthought, a pious theological footnote to an essentially intellectual program.

In *Comus* the role of education in the quest for moral goodness is most clearly illustrated by the Attendant Spirit. Played by the real-life tutor of the Egerton children, Henry Lawes, this tutelary "daemon," as Milton called him in the Trinity manuscript, might appear at first sight to behave rather oddly. For instance, as soon as he becomes aware of his antagonist's imminent arrival, he makes himself "viewless" and proceeds to watch the Lady being deceived into accompanying Comus to his "cottage" (320) without doing anything at all to prevent it. He then apparently listens for some considerable time to her brothers debating the power of chastity before making himself visible again, in the guise of a shepherd, and instructing them how to rescue their sister. And though he seems to be in the lead when he and the brothers set off for Comus's palace—"Thyrsis lead on apace," says the Elder Brother, "Ile follow thee" (657)—he does not arrive there until the crucial confrontation is over: "The Brothers rush in with swords drawn," reads the stage direction, "wrest his Glass out of his hand, and break it against the ground; his rout make sign of resistance, but are all driven in. The Attendant Spirit comes in." Like the angels guarding Eden in *Paradise Lost*, the Attendant Spirit thus seems curiously ineffectual, constantly hovering around the margins of the action but never intervening in it directly. He seems to be determined to avoid encountering his antagonist face-to-face, and he participates only vicariously in the Lady's rescue. He informs, instructs, exhorts, invokes, but he never really acts.

The restrictions Milton places on the Attendant Spirit's activities begin to make sense, however, if we see him as a representative of the humanist educator. For the restrictions are all carefully designed to reveal the limits of education in the moral arena, to demonstrate what can be taught and what cannot. Thus, the reason the Attendant Spirit does not prevent Comus from tempting the Lady is the same as the reason the angels guarding paradise fail to prevent Satan from tempting Adam and Eve: if an individual is to function as a moral agent, he or she must be free to encounter temptation and resist it. If the Attendant Spirit had prevented Comus from leading the Lady off to his palace, or if he had sent her brothers on their rescue mission before Comus had had time to test the Lady's moral character, her virtue would have been "fugitive and cloistered," "unexercised and unbreathed," as Milton was to put it in *Areopagitica* Only if she were permitted to "apprehend and consider vice with all her baits and seeming pleasures, and yet abstain, and yet distinguish, and yet prefer that which is truly better," could she prove herself to be a "true warfaring Christian."[53] As Eve was to ask in *Paradise Lost*, "what is Faith, Love, Vertue unassaid / Alone, without exterior help sustain?" (9.335-36). The function of an educator, Milton believed, was to instruct his students, not to protect them, to inform and advise them, not to guard them. He could coach the players, but he could not enter the playing field himself.

If the Attendant Spirit plays the part of the humanist educator, who then is the representative of divine grace? At first sight the most obvious candidate would appear to be Sabrina, whose intervention is necessary to complete the task begun by the Lady's brothers. Cued by the Attendant Spirit's advice to leave Comus's palace "while heaven lends us grace" (938), most critics of the masque consequently equate the daughter of Locrine in one way or another with the power of divine providence. According to William B. Madsen, to cite just one example of many, whereas the Attendant Spirit "symbolizes the knowledge of right and wrong conferred by reason, she [symbolizes] the power of doing right conferred by grace."[54] Just as Virgil is eventually displaced by Beatrice in the *Divine Comedy*, so the Attendant Spirit gives way to "the Goddess of the River" (842).

Attractive though it may be from a purely conceptual point of view, this equation seems to me to run counter to virtually all the details of Milton's text. As Robert M. Adams has observed, if Sabrina represents grace, "would it not be unreasonable to invoke her by means of a long list of explicitly pagan deities? Would it not be absurd to let her sing about willows, osiers, and cowslips, but not a word about God or grace or divine power, and so to dismiss her to Amphitrite's bower without a single hint dropped as to Christian grace?"[55] Would it not be indecorous, we might add, to embody the power of divine providence in a local water nymph who, according to legend, was the illegitimate offspring of a pre-Christian British king? And quite apart from such artistic considerations, is it likely that a seventeenth-century English Protestant who believed that divine grace was the freely given gift of God would represent it as a response to the Attendant Spirit's "warbled Song" (854)? Like Comus himself, we might also note, Sabrina is more closely associated with the natural order than with the divine—in David Norbrook's words, she "is essentially an image of the beauty and harmony of nature."[56] If she represents anything in addition to the benevolent power of the local environment, then it is surely the response to nature's bounty that Comus had sought to subvert: virginity. As we have already seen, there are two quite distinct temptations in *Comus*, the temptation to intemperance, which is undone by carrying out the Attendant Spirit's instruction to "break his glass, / And shed the lushious liquor on the ground" (651-52), and the temptation to unchastity, which is undone by sprinkling the Lady's breast with drops from Sabrina's "fountain pure" (912). Comus thus has not one but two antagonists: in the masque of temperance his antagonist is the Attendant Spirit, the children's teacher, with whom he shares the shepherd's disguise, a semidivine origin, and a propensity to speak in Jonsonian tetrameters; in the masque of abstinence it is Sabrina, the defender of chastity, with whom he shares a local habitat, a proper name (as opposed to "the Lady," "the Brothers," "the Attendant Spirit"), and a close association with the natural world. And indeed, everything we learn about Sabrina confirms that she represents virginity. A "Virgin pure" herself (826), she loves "maid'nhood" and is always ready to aid "a Virgin such as was herself" (855-56). Her office is "to help ensnared chastity" (909), and she undoes Comus's charm by touching the "marble venom'd seat" with "chaste palms moist and cold" (918).

In fact, the character who is most suited to represent divine grace in the poem is not Sabrina at all, but the Attendant Spirit. Unlike Sabrina, he is a celestial being, whose home is far above the watery element that she inhabits. Unlike Sabrina, he "stoops" from heaven to assist not only "ensnared chastity," but also "any favor'd of high Jove" (78)—perhaps the clearest reference to the doctrine of the Puritan elect in any of Milton's early poems.[57] And most important of all, unlike Sabrina, he does not have to be summoned. As the agent of divine providence, dispatched "by quick command from Soveran Jove" (41), he presides over the entire masque like a benevolent deity, witnessing the Lady's deception by Comus, arming her brothers with "haemony," leading them on their rescue mission, summoning Sabrina when they fail to carry out all his instructions, guiding the children to Ludlow castle, presenting them to their parents, and instructing the audience in the meaning of the events they have just witnessed.

The obvious objection to this interpretation of the Attendant Spirit is the evidence that just led us to identify him as a teacher. If, as I argued earlier, he exemplifies the capacities and limitations of humanist education, how can he simultaneously embody the operations of divine grace? The answer, I want to suggest, is that, in Milton's view at this stage of his life, education is a product of grace and the teacher an instrument of divine providence. Hence the Attendant Spirit's twin identities in the masque. As Thyrsis, the shepherd charged with guarding the Lord President's sheep, he is the fictional counterpart of Henry Lawes, the literal tutor of the Lord President's children. As the Attendant Spirit, however, he is also a supernatural being, a "daemon" who takes the form of a shepherd only in order to fulfill his providential mission.[58] In much the same way, Milton asserted in the *Elegia Quarta* that his own tutor, Thomas Young, was one of those "whom God himself sent, who bring you glad tidings from the skies, who teach you what way, when men are dust, leads them to the stars" (92-94). The representative of education is simultaneously a vehicle for divine grace. Milton could hardly have made his thesis clearer: the knowledge that enables "mortals" to act virtuously is itself a gift from heaven.[59]

But how efficacious was such divinely inspired instruction likely to be in a fallen world? Could imperfect human beings really be taught to "lay their just hands on that Golden Key / That ope's the Palace of Eternity" (*Comus*, 13-14)? The answer to this question is encoded, I believe, in the brothers' behavior and, to a still greater extent, in the Lady's. To put it as simply as possible, the dramatic action implies that though we can be taught to resist temptation—to say no—we cannot be taught to perform a positive act of virtue—to say yes. The brothers may be able to drive Comus out of his palace, but they cannot do him any real harm. As Jeanne Martin has emphasized, he is consequently the only masque villain who lives on to fight another day.[60] Neither the brothers, nor the Attendant Spirit, nor Sabrina can defeat him for good; they can only rescue his potential victims. The Lady, in turn, may be able to reject the poisoned cup and the invitation to promiscuity, but she cannot free herself from her "stony fetters" (819). Her virtue is a virtue of omission, symbolized first by her physical immobility even after her brothers have expelled her tempter and then by her absolute silence once Sabrina has released her. As she sits there, paralyzed and silent, she dramatizes the first two steps of virtue that Lactantius defines in the passage quoted at the beginning of this chapter: she abstains from evil works and she abstains from evil words.[61]

Here, then, is the final and perhaps the most compelling reason for Milton's emphasis on virginity: of all the human virtues, it is the one most suited to exemplify the point he wished to make. For by definition chastity does not consist in doing anything; it consists rather in *not* doing something, and as a result it is perhaps the closest practical metaphor one could find for the kind of virtue Milton believed to be attainable: the virtue of privation. As an ontological tabula rasa, moreover, it had a second attraction. To a far greater extent than any other human property, chastity could serve in the fallen world as a surrogate for the original state of innocence that Adam and Eve enjoyed before the Fall. Virginity was the closest we could come to that prelapsarian condition of perfect sinlessness. In our postlapsarian world we do not merely apprehend good as an absence of evil, as Milton implied in the *Nativity Ode*. Insofar as we achieve good, we do so by rejecting its opposite. In moral as well as in cognitive terms, good is a privation of evil.

3

THE ROAD FROM HORTON

One suggestive metaphor for a developmental crisis is a man alone on a body of water trying to get from Island Past to Island Future. He fears that he will not reach Future. He feels that he can move neither forward nor backward, that he is on the verge of drowning. A man may experience himself as swimming alone, as rowing in a leaky boat, or as captain of a luxurious but defective ship caught in a storm.

—Daniel J. Levinson,
The Seasons of a Man's Life, 86

WHEN HE WROTE *LYCIDAS* in 1637 Milton was almost twenty-nine years old. For the past five years he had been living with his parents, first in Hammersmith and later in the rural village of Horton. Deeply committed to the ideals of studious retirement and sexual abstinence, he was unmarried, unemployed, and relatively unknown. His chief ambition was to be a great poet. During the five years following the composition of *Lycidas* he traveled extensively in France and Italy, took up residence in London, married Mary Powell, and established himself as one of the principal public champions of the Puritan and Parliamentarian cause. With the exception of an occasional sonnet, he did not produce another poem in English until he was almost sixty.

This drastic change in the direction of his life suggests that Milton underwent what Daniel J. Levinson has called an "Age Thirty Transition," a period of personal crisis in which one's past is reappraised and one's future redefined. During the "Age Thirty

Transition," Levinson writes, "the provisional, exploratory quality of the twenties is ending and a man has a sense of greater urgency. . . . He has the feeling: 'If I want to change my life—if there are things in it that I don't like, or things missing that I would like to have—this is the time to make a start, for soon it will be too late.' The Age Thirty Transition provides a 'second chance' to create a more satisfactory life structure within early adulthood."[1] My thesis here is that *Lycidas* records the beginning of such a transition, that it constitutes a crucial Miltonic moment within the poet's own life. Although the interpretation that follows will thus run counter to the prevailing view of *Lycidas* as an impersonal exercise in the conventions of the pastoral elegy, I am not proposing a return to the naively biographical approach of critics like E.M.W. Tillyard and Robert Graves, who virtually ignored the poem's relationship to the generic traditions lying behind it. Indeed, I argue that it was precisely through his dialogue with the pastoral and elegiac traditions that Milton first came face-to-face with the frustrations and anxieties that were to change the future course of his life.

Nor do I wish to suggest that *Lycidas* is a deliberately self-analytical, or even a consciously self-referential, poem. Like so much of Milton's early verse, it is first and foremost an occasional, and to that extent a public, work. Its announced purpose is to mourn the untimely death of Edward King, not to reveal Milton's misgivings about his own career. But beneath the marmoreal formality of the surface, I believe, Milton can be observed in the process of discovering some of his deepest anxieties. The poem is simultaneously a public tribute to a learned friend and an intensely private encounter with the accumulated doubts and fears that would eventually transform the retiring, young, virgin poet of Horton into the publicly outspoken, thrice-married polemicist of Westminster.

In one of the most haunting passages in the poem, Milton describes how the natural landscape reacted to the death of Lycidas:

> But O the heavy change, now thou art gon,
> Now thou art gon, and never must return!

Thee Shepherd, thee the Woods, and desert Caves,
With wilde Thyme and the gadding Vine o'regrown,
And all their echoes mourn. [37-41]

The editors of the *Variorum Commentary* are probably right in detecting a sidelong glance at the myth of Echo and Narcissus in the final phrase, for the "Sweet Queen of Parly," as the Lady calls her in *Comus* (240), is not only present in the repeated clauses and pronouns of the previous four lines; she presides over the entire poem.[2] For instance, Milton begins his elegy with an echo—"Yet once more, 0 ye Laurels, and once more"—and then, when the thought of the Christian resurrection leads him to make a fresh start at line 165, he signals his intention by echoing the echo, rhythmically and verbally—"Weep no more, woful Shepherds weep no more." As Josephine Miles has remarked, *Lycidas* is full of such repetitions:[3] "For *Lycidas* is dead, dead ere his prime, / Young *Lycidas*" (8-9); "Begin then, Sisters of the sacred well, . . . Begin" (15-17); "Together both . . . and both together" (25-27); "The Muse her self that Orpheus bore, / The Muse her self" (58-59); "Return Alpheus . . . Return Sicilian Muse" (132-33); "And now the Sun had stretch'd out all the hills, / And now . . . " (190-91). We might almost be listening to an exercise in the various iterative schemes that the rhetoricians of the period have taught us to recognize. To an even greater degree than Marvell's address to his coy mistress, Milton's tribute to his chaste friend is an "echoing song."

As a result, it sounds very much as if it too were taking place in the kind of "marble vault" that Marvell imagines as the setting for his poem, a hollow burial chamber in which the mourner is the only living human presence. For in addition to the various functions that Peter Sacks has attributed to what he calls "the elegiac convention of repetition," echoic language can communicate a sense of personal isolation and loneliness more powerfully perhaps than any other device at the poet's disposal.[4] In the present instance, the echoes imply that the death of Edward King has left Milton utterly alone. The only human voice to respond to his mourning song is his own.

But there is another kind of echo in the opening lines of the poem, one that reaches far beyond the immediate confines of the text itself. The initial phrase "Yet once more" echoes a well-known passage in the Epistle to the Hebrews that was commonly associated with the prophecies of the Second Coming and the Day of Judgement in Revelation: "Yet once more I shake not the earth only, but also heaven. And this word, Yet once more, signifieth the removing of those things that are shaken" (12:26-27).[5] And the ensuing description of plucking the laurels and the myrtles rephrases a line from Virgil's second *Eclogue:* "You too, O laurels, I will pluck, and you their neighbour myrtle" (54). As generations of editors from Thomas Newton to A.S.P. Woodhouse have pointed out, Milton's elegy resonates throughout with such allusions. Beginning with the actual title, direct and indirect references to other works combine to create a context so dense with association that *Lycidas* appears to be a much larger poem in retrospect than it really is. As the moments of recognition accumulate, the text gradually expands in our minds until we have the paradoxical sense that it contains the tradition to which it belongs. The experience of reading Milton's tribute to Edward King is consequently a good deal more strenuous than that of reading anything else he had written up to this point in his career. We seem to be engaged in an activity that is simultaneously receptive and creative, as if the completed poem were at least partly the product of our own literary-historical sensibilities. And so in a way it is, for the chamber in which all the echoes finally congregate is the reader's harmonizing memory.

In substantive as well as in formal terms, then, repetition is of the very essence in this work. Everything in *Lycidas*, one could say without too much exaggeration, happens twice—including the repetitions themselves, which often turn out to be echoes of echoes, as in the case of line 165, or allusions to allusions, as in the case of the address to the nymphs. Indeed, the entire poem is a kind of recurrence: "Yet once more . . ."

This phenomenon is hardly surprising when we recall how deeply the idea of repetition was ingrained in the cultural consciousness of the Renaissance. The period as a whole defined itself as a revival of an earlier civilization, and this self-perception was reflected in turn by the basic imperative of the educational system: the imitation of the ancients. As a product of that system, Milton not only revitalized the major classical genres; he seems at times to have thought of himself as reliving the actual experiences of the classical authors, notably those of Virgil.

As the foregoing examples suggest, however, repetitions are rarely, if ever, exact, particularly literary ones. For by virtue of the simple fact that they occur in new contexts, restatements inevitably modify their originals in one way or another. The second time is never quite the same as the first. In the case of biblical typology, for instance, the Old Testament figures are completed rather than merely duplicated by their New Testament fulfillments. In *Paradise Regained* the second Adam thus initiates the redemption of the human race by living out in the Galilean wilderness a perfected version of the first Adam's brief sojourn in the garden of Eden. "For as by one man's disobedience many were made sinners; so by the obedience of one shall many be made righteous."[6] So superior was the fulfillment to its figure, indeed, that the relationship beween the two was frequently assumed to be essentially antithetical. Opposite the Old Testament types stood the New Testament antitypes. Nor was this contrastive approach confined to the interpretation of the Bible. As I observed in chapter 1, the legends of classical Greece and Rome could also be read as reverse images of scriptural truths, pagan fictions destined to be corrected by Christian facts. For the Christian humanists of the Renaissance, the Virgin Mary was an antitype not only of Eve but of Venus.

In much the same way, the recurrences in *Lycidas* often turn out to be inversions rather than simple reiterations of their antecedents. The weary "once more" of the first line gives way to a triumphant "no more" as Milton announces King's resurrection. "For Lycidas is dead" (8) is eventually canceled by "For Lycidas your sorrow is not dead" (166), while the twice-repeated downward movement of "sunk so low" (102) and "Sunk though he be" (167) suddenly turns upward with the concluding assertion that the dead shepherd is "sunk low, but mounted high" (172). Like true mirror images, the internal echoes in *Lycidas* transpose what they reproduce. In a world containing "Blind mouthes" (119), the logic of the poem persuades us, it is only natural that there should also be eyes that "suck" (140).

The same basic pattern is also observable in the way the external echoes operate. Over and over again what strikes us is not so much the appropriateness as the glaring inappropriateness of Milton's allusions to the works of his predecessors. The more we learn about the various figures the poet marshals for comparison with Edward King, the less they appear to resemble him. Lycidas himself, as we shall see below, was usually the mourner in pastoral elegies; here he is the deceased. Gallus, whose ghost accompanies Lycidas throughout the poem, was a famous lover; his seventeenth-century counterpart dies chaste. And Orpheus, King's mythic surrogate in the poem, was murdered by the Bacchantes; Milton's "hapless youth" died by accident. Each *déjà vue* thus proves to be, on closer inspection, a *vue renversée*. We are being persuaded by the poem's allusive strategy to look backward in more senses than one.

My chief contention in the following pages will be that reversal is the basic structural principle at work in *Lycidas*, that the casual antimetabole with which the poet identifies himself with his subject—"Together both . . . and both together" (25-27)—enacts in miniature the strategy of the entire poem. Thematically, as Richard P. Adams and others have demonstrated, the elegy develops an elaborate antithesis between the concepts of death and rebirth.[7] Generically, as I argue later, *Lycidas* illustrates Harold Bloom's dictum that "poetic influence—when it involves two strong, authentic poets,—always proceeds by a misreading of the prior poet, an act of creative correction that is actually and necessarily a misinterpretation."[8] Milton's poem, that is to say, seems to have been written *against* the tradition of the pastoral elegy, *contra* such poems as Theocritus's first *Idyl* and Virgil's tenth *Eclogue*. And psychologically, as I show in the final section of this chapter, *Lycidas* marks a dramatic turning point in Milton's own career, a "decisive instant" that eventuated in a major reversal in his values and in the subsequent course of his life. Despite its initial rejection of "denial" (18), *Lycidas* is one long act of contradiction.

The seventeenth century took the business of titles seriously, so when a contemporary reader came to the final poem in *Justa Edouardo King Naufrago*, the first question to arise might well have been: why Lycidas? The opening lines would immediately have supplied a partial answer: because the name is redolent of pastoral, and Milton's contribution to the volume, unlike the others, is a pastoral elegy. But though this narrows the question somewhat, it does not dispose of it altogether, for one could still ask, with Louis L. Martz, "[W]hy, of all the pastoral names available, should Milton have chosen that one name Lycidas?"[9] According to the editors of the *Variorum Commentary*, "there seems to be no special significance in the choice," and indeed, to the best of my knowledge, Martz's is the only serious attempt to discover any.[10] Yet Milton was not in the habit of naming his works arbitrarily. We know from the evidence of the drafts in the Trinity Manuscript that he considered at least three possible titles for *Paradise Lost* before settling upon his original version. If he chose to call Edward King by one pastoral pseudonym rather than another, he is likely to have had a good reason for doing so.

The task of discovering that reason is complicated by the sheer popularity of the particular pseudonym he selected. According to Watson Kirkconnell, a reading of W.L. Grant's *Neo-Latin Literature and the Pastoral* yielded no fewer than thirty-two "Lycidas's in Latin pastoral alone," and a study of Greek, Italian, and English sources would probably add as many instances again.[11] Fortunately, however, Milton himself has provided a clue that may serve to reduce the potential evidence to manageable proportions. In his very next elegy, the *Epitaphium Damonis*, he describes his visit to Florence in the following terms: "Oh, how wondrous great was I, when, stretched at ease by the prattlings of the cool Arno, in its poplar grove, where the grass was softest, I could pluck now violets, now the tips of the myrtles, and could hear Menalcas vying with Lycidas!" (129-32). The reference to competition points towards Theocritus's seventh *Idyl*, in which a goatherd called Lycidas engages in a singing match with Simichidas. The identification of his competitor as Menalcas, on the other hand, recalls Virgil's ninth *Eclogue*, in which Lycidas, now a shepherd, discusses with Moeris the poetic achievement of a friend bearing that name.[12] It was these two poems, I believe, that Milton intended his audience to bring to mind when he called his earlier elegy *Lycidas*.

Milton's simultaneous allusion to them in the *Epitaphium Damonis* is not, of course, the only connection between the seventh *Idyl* and the ninth *Eclogue*. As Michael C.J. Putnam has pointed out, the Latin work closely resembles the Greek in setting, if not in theme.[13] For instance, though neither of them is an elegy, each takes place in the immediate vicinity of a grave. When Simichidas meets Lycidas at the beginning of the *Idyl* he is almost within sight of the tomb of Brasilas, and when Lycidas and Moeris finish their conversation in the *Eclogue* the tomb of Bianor is just coming into view. We are only one step removed from the situation in Poussin's *Et in Arcadia ego*, or from the scene that Milton wistfully conjures up in *Lycidas:*

> So may some gentle Muse
> With lucky words favour my destin'd Urn,
> And as he passes turn,
> And bid fair peace be to my sable shrowd. [19-22]

Nor is this the only similarity between the two classical poems. In both, the encounter with Lycidas occurs in the middle of a journey. Theocritus's characters are en route from the city to the country, Virgil's from the country to the city. For the duration of their respective dialogues, the characters are suspended in a kind of metaphorical no man's land between the urban and the pastoral worlds. As a result, one has a strong sense of hiatus, of arrested movement, as if the poems themselves were interruptions in a process of transition that cannot be completed until they are over. Milton's *Lycidas*, I shall argue, occupies a very similar position in his personal journey along the road from Horton to Westminster.

Taken individually, the *Idyl* and the *Eclogue* bear still more directly on Milton's elegy. To begin with the former, what makes it so specifically relevant is the actual song that Lycidas offers as his entry in the contest with Simichidas:

> Ageanax will have a fair voyage to Mitylene, even when
> the Kids are in the west and the south wind drives the
> wet waves and when Orion holds his feet on the ocean,
> if he will but set free Lycidas, who is burned by
> Aphrodite, since a hot love for him consumes me. The
> halcyons will still the waves, and the sea and the south

wind and the east wind, which stirs the seaweed on the highest shore—the halcyons, which are of all birds most beloved by the sea-green Nereids, of all those birds which take their prey from the sea. As Ageanax makes his voyage to Mitylene, may all be favorable to him, and may he reach harbor after a happy journey.[14]

The irony of naming "a learned Friend, unfortunately drown'd in his passage from Chester on the Irish Seas" after a shepherd who bade his lover a safe voyage across the Aegean is too exact to be accidental.[15]

We never find out whether Lycidas's protective song in the *Idyl* has had the desired effect, but the relaxed and light-hearted tone of the work as a whole suggests that Ageanax did indeed arrive safely at his destination. In Virgil's ninth *Eclogue*, on the other hand, the power of poetry to shape events is called into serious question. Commenting on Lycidas's opening speech in that poem, Putnam writes: "If chance overturns all things . . . will the poet's song have the ability to reverse the workings of fortune and save everything? Can poetry, intimate and crucial part of bucolic life that it is, preserve it from destruction?"[16] Virgil's answer, as he goes on to argue, is a qualified "no." At first, Lycidas is surprised by the news that Moeris has been expelled from his lands; he had heard a rumor that "your Menalcas had with his songs saved all" (10). But Moeris quickly disabuses him of any such fanciful notions: "You had heard, and so the story ran," he replies, "but amid the weapons of war, Lycidas, our songs avail as much as, they say, the doves of Chaonia when the eagle comes" (11-12). Together the two shepherds then attempt to recall some of their favorite songs, only to discover that they can no longer recollect them in their entirety. "The measure I remember," remarks Lycidas as he tries to recite Moeris's apostrophe to Daphnis, "could I but keep the words" (45). Moeris's reply anticipates the "mere oblivion" of melancholy Jaques's portrayal of old age. "Time robs us of all, even of memory," he declares. "Now I have forgotten all my songs. Even voice itself now fails Moeris" (51-54). Death is clearly not far off, and it is no accident that in the next speech Lycidas announces that they are arriving at a tomb.

The contrast with the *Idyl* is striking. Gone is the buoyant optimism of Theocritus's characters, and with it their confidence in the efficacy of their own poetic talents. Lycidas and Moeris are no Vladimir and Estragon—the master they are waiting for really exists—but the setting in which Virgil has placed them is almost as inimical to the human imagination as the desolate world of Beckett's play. As Putnam says, "*Idyl* 7 is a poem about joy in song, about the beauty and variety of poetry, set in the context of a journey to a haven of particular beauty. The ninth *Eclogue* is opposite in tone and meaning. Virgil's road leads not toward the glorious retreat of a harvest festival but out of the country in the direction of the city, through a landscape where song is impossible."[17]

Once again the relevance to Milton's *Lycidas* is subtle but direct, for one of the major issues raised by the death of Edward King has to do with the value of poetry in a society that has been deafened by the "hideous roar" (61) of Bacchic revelers or corrupted by the "lean and flashy songs" (123) of faithless shepherds. Writing in the aftermath of a civil war that had deprived him of his farm, Virgil had pondered the worth of the poetic vocation. Writing during the prelude to a civil war that was to absorb most of his energies for the following decade, Milton is faced with the same question. If the muse is not only thankless but powerless to boot, then what is the point of serving her so strictly? If songs are of no avail among the weapons of war, then what is the point of singing them? For Milton's classically trained audience, then, the mere title of *Lycidas* would have been enough to evoke a whole complex of ideas and associations that look forward to one of the central themes in the body of the poem, the validity of the poetic vocation.

A reader whose memory of classical pastoral had already been triggered by the poem's title would have been unlikely to miss Milton's unusually prolonged and specific allusion to another classical eclogue during the remainder of the elegy. As Milton's editors unfailingly remind us, *Lycidas* is closely modeled on Virgil's tenth *Eclogue*, itself a free adaptation of Theocritus's first *Idyl*.[18] Set in Arcadia, Virgil's poem commemorates the death of the famous soldier, statesman, and poet Cornelius Gallus, whose mistress,

Lycoris, has deserted him for another man. After a short prologue setting the scene, the formal lament begins by asking, "What groves, what glades were your abode, ye virgin Naiads, when Gallus was pining with a love unrequited? For no heights of Parnassus or of Pindus, no Aonian Aganippe made you tarry" (9-12). Virgil then proceeds to describe a series of visitors who arrive to comfort or to admonish Gallus as he lies at the brink of death. Apollo, the god of poetry, urges him to forget his mistress: "Gallus, what madness is this? Thy sweetheart Lycoris hath followed another amid snows and amid rugged camps" (21-23). A rustic deity called Silvanus arrives waving fennel flowers and tall lilies. And Pan, the god of shepherds, advises Gallus to stop grieving: "Will there be no end? Love recks naught of this; neither is cruel Love sated with tears, nor the grass with the rills, nor bees with clover, nor goats with leaves" (28-30). But despite these reproaches, Gallus continues to love the unfaithful Lycoris and with his last words affirms the sovereignty of Eros: "Love conquers all; let us, too, yield to Love" (69).

Together with Virgil's other eclogues this poem was a standard fixture in the curriculum of seventeenth-century grammar schools, and most, if not all, of Milton's readers would have been intimately familiar with it. Virgil, they would have learned from their school texts, wrote the poem not to celebrate the value of love but to warn us against its insidious power. "In this Eclogue," declared one contemporary authority, "is set forth the picture of a foolish lover, so that by looking at this picture we may learn to avoid all the occasions and enticements by which this fire is wont to be aroused."[19] According to the Renaissance schoolmaster John Brinsley, Gallus could have cured himself "by giving his mind to the studie of Poetrie," but he failed to do so. Thus, when Virgil asked the nymphs where they were while Gallus was dying, he was really rebuking the Muses "that they were so carelesse of Gallus to let him so leave his studies and to perish in such unbeseeming love."[20] Like the fourth book of the *Aeneid*, then, the tenth *Eclogue* was read in the Renaissance as an example of the distracting power of love. "Omnia vincit Amor" was a warning, not an affirmation.

Other commentators, noting Gallus's career as a statesman, found in him "a memorable example of the kind of fortune one gets at court" and interpreted Virgil's questions to the nymphs in political terms.[21] Parnassus and Pindus, wrote William Lisle, "were the places of Gallus his retrait amongst the Muses, and to the study of sweete Poesie: wherein if hee had still retir'd himselfe, and had not aspired to the great Imployments, and Business of state, which caus'd his ruin, hee had still liv'd."[22] According to this view of the poem, Virgil's lament for Gallus was a warning against the perils of politics.

The resemblances between *Eclogue X* and *Lycidas* are striking and numerous. Phoebus Apollo appears at a crucial juncture in both poems. Virgil's Silvanus, wearing "rustic glories on his brow, waving his fennel flowers and tall lilies" (24-25), is clearly the prototype of Milton's Camus, with his "Mantle hairy, and his Bonnet sedge, / Inwrought with figures dim" (104-5). Pan, the god of shepherds, has his counterpart in Peter, the founder of the church. Both poems ask the same question, Virgil's "Who would refuse verses to Gallus?" (3) being echoed by Milton's "Who would not sing for Lycidas?" (10). Both poems appeal to Arethusa for aid. Both poems interrogate the nymphs, though Milton substitutes British for Arcadian landmarks in his adaptation of Virgil's lines:

> Where were ye Nymphs when the remorseless deep
> Clos'd o'er the head of your lov'd Lycidas?
> For neither were ye playing on the steep,
> Where your old Bards, the famous Druids, ly,
> Nor on the shaggy top of Mona high,
> Nor yet where Deva spreads his wisard stream. [50-55]

And both poems conclude with the image of a shepherd rising to his feet at evening and setting off for home with his flock.

But striking as they are, these formal resemblances pale beside the substantive difference between the heroes of the two elegies. Unlike Gallus, Edward King had remained chaste all his life, thereby earning the right, reserved for those who "were not defiled with women," of participating in the marriage of the Lamb.[23] Amaryllis and Neaera were never able to make him break his vow "to scorn delights, and live laborious dayes" (72). His only mistress was his muse. And unlike Gallus, he did not abandon his studies in order to pursue a political career. He had meditated his maker no less "strictly" (66) than his muse.

We might well conclude, therefore, that Gallus functions in this poem in much the same way that Achilles and Ulysses function in *Paradise Lost:* as a counterfigure, whose pagan imperfections define the Christian virtue of Milton's hero. But there may be rather more to the matter than that, for there is one final difference between Edward King and his classical predecessor that totally transforms the significance of all the rest: in Peter Sacks's words, "King's death was an accident—there was no one to blame."[24] It simply could not be attributed, as Gallus's had been, to some fatal error on his part. He had neither sported in the shade nor striven in the field; he had neither fallen in love nor succumbed to the lures of the court. On the contrary, he had obeyed all the rules that the protagonist of the *Eclogue* had broken, yet he had still been cut off "ere his prime" (8). Hence the bitterness of Milton's criticism of his own version of the address to the nymphs: "Ay me, I fondly dream! / Had ye bin there—for what could that have don?" (56-57). Hence, too, the ensuing allusion to Orpheus's solitary period of abstinence after the death of Eurydice. If a life of austere dedication to poetry was no guarantee of survival, if the "Fury" was really "blind" (75), then what was the point of sexual and political self-denial, what did it "boot" to "tend the homely slighted Shepherds trade" (64-65)?

The contrasts I have noted between Gallus and Edward King could hardly have afforded Milton much comfort, then. They may have demonstrated King's superiority over his predecessor, but they must also have called into question the very standards by which that superiority was measured. The primary allusive context within which Milton chose to lament the fate of his fellow student, therefore, may have served to trigger his anxieties not about the possibility of his own premature death, as Tillyard has suggested, but rather about the validity of the "fugitive and cloistered virtue" advocated by the commentators on Virgil, and, still more to the point, about the validity of the kind of life he himself had been leading since he had retired to his father's rural estate at Horton. In Boccaccio's *Life of Dante*, which Milton had recently been reading, the poet's downfall was attributed to his involvement in the political and amorous affairs of Florence. The fate of Edward King, however, seemed to suggest that Boccaccio had overestimated the efficacy of chastity and retirement. Perhaps there was something to be said for the active life of sexual and political engagement after all.

Gallus is not actually mentioned by name in *Lycidas*. Like Venus and Bacchus, whose myrtle and ivy Milton had invoked in the opening lines, he is an invisible but felt presence in the poem's associative hinterland. The anxieties that the Renaissance interpretation of his story must have aroused in Milton at this particular point of his career could not, however, be left in the background with him. The poet's doubts about the efficacy of chastity and retirement needed an immediate and effective outlet if they were not to undermine the remainder of the elegy. They found it in the figure whose death Milton recalls in the very next lines:

> Ay me, I fondly dream!
> Had ye bin there—for what could that have don?
> What could the Muse her self that Orpheus bore,
> The Muse her self, for her inchanting son
> Whom Universal nature did lament,
> When by the rout that made the hideous roar,
> His goary visage down the stream was sent,
> Down the swift Hebrus to the Lesbian shore. [56-63]

In a pioneering article published in 1949 Caroline W. Mayerson declared that this allusion was a "lost metaphor."[25] One could hardly make the same claim today. Detailed investigations by such scholars as Thomas H. Cain, C. Davidson, Richard J. DuRocher, J.B. Friedman, John Hollander, D.P. Walker, and Marilyn Williamson, not to mention Mayerson herself, have disclosed the wealth of interpretations that the Orpheus legend had accumulated by the time it reached the Renaissance, while intensive scrutiny by such critics as Richard P. Adams, G.S. Fraser, Northrop Frye, and Rosemond Tuve has yielded a wide variety of ingenious explanations of the role played in *Lycidas* by the Thracian singer.[26] The lost metaphor has been comprehensively regained, or so it would seem. Yet in spite of all the attention it has received over the past fifty years or so, Milton's allusion to Orpheus has still not been fully understood.

Three explanations have been offered for the appearance of the Thracian singer at this point in the elegy. According to Tuve, Milton introduced him into the poem in order to show that "nothing is exempt [from death], not man's dearest hope or highest achievement; the principle of death in the universe has worsted what he thought confirmed his immortality, and nothing can outwit, nothing negate, that dark power."[27] Adams, Frye, and Mayerson draw rather less pessimistic inferences from the allusion, finding in it "a hint that Lycidas' recompense may parallel Orpheus'," that he too will experience a form of "salvation out of water" analogous to the rebirth of Adonis at Byblos.[28] And G.S. Fraser, reviving (albeit unwittingly) a widespread medieval interpretation of Orpheus's descent into the underworld, suggests that "he is also a kind of prefiguration of Christ. Like Christ he descends into Hell and comes out again; but, where Christ harrows Hell, Orpheus loses Eurydice at the last moment. . . . Like Christ he is cruelly sacrificed, but, unlike Christ, he has no resurrection."[29]

All three readings of the episode seem to me to be defective in one way or another. The first, as I shall show, fails to take into account what is arguably the most essential factor linking Lycidas with Orpheus. The second and third are open to the rather more obvious objection that they are based upon precisely those elements in the original myth that Milton chose to leave out, namely, Orpheus's attempt to rescue Eurydice from the realm of Pluto and the fate of his head after it had reached "the Lesbian shore" (63). In omitting the first episode, at least, Milton was typical of his age. For whereas medieval authors generally emphasized the quest for Eurydice, with its obvious christological and moral overtones, Renaissance poets and dramatists tended to focus their attention on the latter part of the story, which furnished them with a vivid illustration of the power of song to control both physical and psychological reality.[30] Although this theme was present in the myth from the very beginning, it was the humanists of the fifteenth and sixteenth centuries who, in Thomas H. Cain's words, brought

Orpheus "to his fullest development as a prototype of the compellingly articulate man, the glorified orator or poet."[31] By the time Shakespeare composed the deceptively simple lyric that opens Act III of *Henry VIII*, the tradition of seeing Orpheus "as a model of the poet's powers" was well established:[32]

> Orpheus with his lute made trees
> And the mountain tops that freeze,
> Bow themselves when he did sing;
> To his music plants and flowers
> Ever sprung, as sun and showers
> There had made a lasting spring.
>
> Everything that heard him play,
> Even the billows of the sea,
> Hung their heads and then lay by.
> In sweet music is such art,
> Killing care and grief of heart
> Fall asleep and hearing die. [1-12]

Like the angelic choir in the *Nativity Ode*, the Muse's son can restore the age of gold with his redemptive song.

If Milton's omission of Orpheus's adventures in the underworld was in accord with current attitudes to the legend,[33] however, his emphasis on the Bacchantes' assault and the Muse's impotence was highly unorthodox. The author of *Lycidas*, Mayerson remarks in passing, "appears to be unique among his contemporaries and predecessors in making a poetic adaptation of the death of Orpheus."[34] The point is more important, I think, than she herself seems to have recognized. For by focusing upon the one episode in Orpheus's career which suggested that in the final analysis poetry was powerless to affect history, Milton was not just expressing his poetic originality; he was giving the lie to one of the most revered beliefs in European literary culture.

He was also rejecting his own interpretation of the story in such earlier works as *L'Allegro*, *Il Penseroso*, and *Ad Patrem*, where the Thracian singer appears in his conventional Renaissance guise as "a symbol of poetry's power to control and civilize."[35] The allusion to Orpheus in the last of these poems is particularly interesting in connection with *Lycidas*, for the Latin epistle is clearly related to the English elegy in a number of ways, most significantly by its concern with the nature and worth of the poetic vocation.[36] As critics are fond of saying, *Ad Patrem* is Milton's *Defence of Poetry*. In view of the general line of defense he pursues, it might equally well be called his *Canonization*, for just as Donne refuses to "observe his honour, or his grace, / Or the king's reall, or his stamped face" (6-7), so Milton rejects "the golden hope of storing away money" and "the laws, the ill-guarded statutes of our nation" (70-72); just as Donne retires to the "hermitage" of perfectly fulfilled sexuality, so Milton takes refuge from "the uproar of the city" in "seclusions deep . . . amid the delightful leisure of the Aonian stream," where he can walk "a blessed comrade at Apollo's side" (74-76). The only difference is that the Puritan poet determines to abandon the world of commerce and politics for the sake not of love but of literature. In the Arcadian security of his studies at Horton, he asserts, he will be invulnerable to the ills that afflict those who have chosen to pursue wealth or public office: "Keep yourselves far away, wakeful Cares, keep yourselves far away, Complaints, and the eye of Envy with its crooked leer. Stretch not wide, merciless Calumny, your snake-bearing jaws. Most loathsome crew, you possess naught of baneful power against me, nor am I in your control. Safe, with breast secure, I shall stride on, uplifted high from your viper blows" (105-10).

This boundless confidence in the Muse's capacity to protect her followers from the hostility of a corrupt society is matched only by Milton's faith in her followers' capacity to persuade that society to act less corruptly. There is virtually nothing, he assures his father, that human eloquence cannot accomplish when it is divinely inspired. Poets are the acknowledged legislators of the world, and their original prototype is Orpheus, "who by his songs . . . held fast the streams, and added ears to the oaks by his songs . . . and by his singing compelled to tears the shades that were done with life" (52-55).

It is a far cry from this majestic figure to the helpless victim of "the rout that made the hideous roar" (61). Even though they both derive from the original myth, the Orpheus whose song could make rivers stand still in *Ad Patrem* and the Orpheus whose "goary visage down the stream was sent" (62) in *Lycidas* are scarcely recognizable as the same character. The one seems to belong to the sunlit landscapes of Theocritus's seventh *Idyl*, the other to the joyless and decaying world of Virgil's ninth *Eclogue*.[37] Milton could hardly have given us a more precise or vivid way of measuring the impact that the death of Edward King must have had upon his conception of the poetic vocation. The youthful optimism that had animated the epistle to his father has collapsed in a nightmare of senseless destruction, which even the Muse was powerless to prevent. Critics who, like Adams and Fraser, insist on superimposing upon that vision the less gloomy aspects of the Orpheus legend do violence not only to the text of *Lycidas* but to the intensity of Milton's desperation at this juncture of the poem. Of the three readings of the episode I summarized earlier, only Tuve's recognizes the profound pessimism that informs Milton's allusion to the Muse's "inchanting son" (59).

What Tuve's interpretation does not recognize is the fundamental source of Milton's pessimism, which has to do not so much with the fact of Orpheus's death as with the circumstances surrounding it. Ovid describes them as follows:

> Throughout this time [that is, after his failure to rescue Eurydice] Orpheus had shrunk from loving any woman, either because of his unhappy experience, or because he had pledged himself not to do so. In spite of this there were many who were fired with a desire to marry the poet, many who were indignant to find themselves repulsed. However, Orpheus preferred to centre his affections on boys of tender years, and to enjoy the brief spring and early flowering of their youth; he was the first to introduce this custom among the people of Thrace. . . . Looking down from the crest of a hill, the female followers of Bacchus, with animal skins slung across their breasts, saw Orpheus as he was singing and accompanying himself on the lyre. One of them, tossing her hair till it streamed in the light breeze, cried out: "See! Look here! Here is the man who scorns us!"

and flung her spear at the poet Apollo loved, at the lips
which produced such melodies. . . . All their weapons
would have been rendered harmless by the charm of
Orpheus' songs, but clamorous shouting, Phrygian
flutes with curving horns, tambourines, the beating of
breasts, and Bacchic howlings, drowned the music of
the lyre. Then at last the stones grew crimson with the
blood of the poet, whose voice they did not hear. . . .
Hurling their leaf-decked thyrsi, made for a far differ-
ent purpose, the women launched their attack on the
poet. . . . Dead to all reverence, they tore him apart
and, through those lips to which rocks had listened,
which wild beasts had understood, his last breath slipped
away and vanished in the wind.[38]

Critics of *Lycidas* have persistently refused to acknowledge that
the mainspring of this part of the Orpheus legend is the theme
of sexual (or, more precisely, of heterosexual) abstinence.
Mayerson's summary of the story bowdlerizes its most crucial
element—"retreated from society" hardly does justice to Ovid's
explicit description of Orpheus's misogyny—and the explanation
in the *Variorum Commentary* is equally mealy-mouthed. "After
his final loss of Eurydice," we are told, "Orpheus roamed his
native Thrace, lamenting his loss and charming with his song all
nature, animate and inanimate. Enraged by his devotion to his
dead wife and his implied scorn of them, the frenzied Maenads
attacked him."[39]

Medieval commentators, though clearly embarrassed by the
pederastic inclinations of one of their favorite Christ-figures, were
at least willing to confront Ovid's text in its entirety. Taking their
cue from Boethius, who had interpreted Orpheus's love for
Eurydice as an example of reason's submission to passion, they
allegorized his subsequent distaste for women as a victory over
carnal concupiscence.[40] On account of the loss of Eurydice, wrote
Giovanni del Virgilio, "Orpheus renounced Hell, that is, tempta-
tion, and reconciling himself to God began to spurn women, giv-
ing his soul instead to God, and began to love men, that is, to act
in a manly way, on which account he was dead to the delights of

the world; for such men are dead to the world."[41] And Arnulf of Orleans explained that Orpheus "shunned women, that is, those acting in a womanlike manner, drunkards and vicious men, but transferred his love to men, that is, to those acting in a manly way."[42]

By the seventeenth century this moralistic reading of the episode had coalesced with Boccaccio's humanistic interpretation of the conclusion of the story, according to which the snake stood for "the circling years . . . which tried to devour Orpheus' head—that is, his name or rather those works Orpheus composed by his genius . . . while the powers of imagination throve in his head. The snake is said to be turned into stone, however, to show that time can in no way put Orpheus down."[43] The result was the characteristic Renaissance version of the legend to be found in Bacon's *Wisdom of the Ancients* and Sandys's commentary on the *Metamorphoses*. Orpheus was averse to women, they both argued, because "the sweets of marriage and the dearness of children commonly draw men away from performing great and lofty services to the commonwealth; being content to be perpetuated in their race and stock, and not in their deeds."[44]

For most of Milton's readers, then, the Muse's son was not simply a poet. He was a poet who, in Sandys's words, judged "the propagation of wisdom and virtuous endeavours" by means of poetry to be "more noble and immortall than that of posterity."[45] This is precisely how Milton himself had described Orpheus in the *Elegia Sexta* just eight years before the composition of *Lycidas:*

> but if a poet sings of wars, of Heaven controlled by a Jove full grown, of duty-doing heroes, of captains that are half gods, if he sings now the holy counsels of the gods above, now the realms below wherein howls a savage hound, let him live a simple frugal life, after the fashion of the teacher who came from Samos, let herbs offer him food that works no harm, let pellucid water stand near him, in a tiny cup of beechen wood, and let him drink only sober draughts from a pure spring. On such a poet are imposed, too, a youth free of crime, pure and chaste, and a character unyielding, and a name

without taint; such an one must he be as you are, augur, as, resplendent with holy vestments and with lustral waters, you rise, minded to go forth to face the angry gods. In this way, story says, wise Tiresias lived, after the light had been swept away from him, and Ogygian Linus, and Calchas, exiled from his hearth, . . . and aged Orpheus, in the lonely grots, after he had tamed the wild beasts. [55-70]

In Milton's eyes, as in those of his contemporaries, Orpheus was an exemplar not only of poetic eloquence but of the abstemiousness necessary to achieve it.

It was this aspect of the myth that I had in mind when I claimed earlier that Tuve's commentary fails to take account of the most crucial factor linking Orpheus with Edward King. For what the Greek poet and his seventeenth-century successor have in common is their refusal to sport with Amaryllis in the shade, and what makes their deaths so profoundly disquieting to Milton is the inability of their innocence to keep the blind fury at bay. Although his devotion to chastity was no doubt as sincere as that of the Lady in *Comus*, no "glistring Guardian" descended to keep King's life "unassail'd" (*Comus*, 218-19), while Orpheus's newly won abstinence, far from dashing "brute violence" (*Comus*, 450), apparently provoked it. The son of Calliope was "torne in peeces by women," explained Thomas Cooper in his *Dictionarium Historicum et Poeticum*, "*because* that for the sorow of his wyfe Eurydice he did not onely himselfe refuse the love of many women, and lyved a sole lyfe, but also disswaded others from the company of women."[46] Coming immediately after the address to the nymphs, with its implicit suggestion that by renouncing the pleasures of the flesh one may be able to escape the fate of a Gallus, Milton's reference to Orpheus's death thus serves as a devastating counterexample.[47] For as we have seen, the point of the *ubi eratis* topos in the sixteenth and seventeenth centuries was not so much the saving power of the Muses as the saving power of chastity and retirement. If only the protagonist of the tenth *Eclogue* had not succumbed to "unbeseeming love," he might have survived to write more poetry, or so the commentators believed.[48] The gruesome scene on the banks of the Hebrus totally subverts this simple-minded faith in the efficacy of pastoral virtue. Despite their determination to scorn delights and live laborious days, both Orpheus and his seventeenth-century counterpart had gone "down the stream" (62) anyway. As Peter Sacks has put it, "the economy of sacrifice and reward has collapsed."[49]

Tuve is only partly right, therefore, when she states that the function of the allusion is to remind us "that deathless poetry is not deathless, that nothing is."[50] To the author of the *Elegia Sexta*, *Ad Patrem*, and *Comus*, the most appalling thing about the death of Orpheus must surely have been its injustice rather than its inevitability. The self-denial that Milton had always assumed to be a prerequisite for writing great poetry could evidently have the very same consequences as the sensual indulgence that brought Daphnis and Gallus to their untimely ends. Atropos did not distinguish between bucolic innocence and courtly vice. "Et in Arcadia ego."

The bitter questions that follow the Orpheus episode have often been called digressive, as though they had little or nothing to do with the rest of the poem. But once the real nature of the Orpheus allusion has been recognized, it should be readily apparent that Milton's misgivings about the worth of the homely slighted shepherd's trade are anything but a sudden or unexpected interruption. On the contrary, as Richard DuRocher has observed, they are the logical culmination of a train of thought that began with the address to the nymphs.[51] If in fact it makes no difference whether one obeys or disobeys the rules traditionally associated with Gallus and exemplified by the latter part of Orpheus's career, then the questions Milton asks are not merely relevant; they are inescapable:

> Alas! What boots it with uncessant care
> To tend the homely slighted Shepherds trade,
> And strictly meditate the thankless Muse?
> Were it not better don as others use,
> To sport with Amaryllis in the shade,
> Or with the tangles of Neaera's hair? [64-69]

The sense of release in these lines is almost as powerful as their simultaneous sense of angry bafflement. Like Arethusa's stream, the undercurrent of anxiety that has slowly been gathering strength beneath the allusions to Gallus and Orpheus has finally broken through to the surface.

That it should prove to be such intensely sexual anxiety should come as no surprise after all the doubts that those allusions have tacitly directed at the ideal of chastity. Once again "the sage / And serious doctrine of Virginity" (*Comus*, 785-86) is under attack, but its assailant is no longer a mere belly-god with his cup of cordial julep; it is the blind Fury with her shears, and what is at stake on this occasion is not the honor of an earl's daughter but the future career of an epic poet. Milton's sustained outburst of self-interrogation challenges the fundamental principle upon which his whole conception of the poetic vocation had been based: the denial of the flesh. In a youthful sonnet to the nightingale he had assured the bird that "Whether the Muse, or Love call thee his mate, / Both them I serve, and of their train am I" (13-14). Long before he wrote *Lycidas*, however, he had come to believe that such a divided loyalty was impossible, and had abandoned Love in order to serve the Muse more faithfully. Once she had proved to be as "thankless" (66) as the "cruel-fair" of the courtly tradition, he could hardly avoid wondering whether he had made the right choice. Perhaps, after all, the suppression of the erotic impulse was too high a price to pay for an art he might never survive to practice.[52] At last the issue originally adumbrated by the juxtaposition of Apollo's laurel and Venus's myrtle in the opening lines of the poem is out in the open. What possible justification can there be for worshiping the god of poetry to the exclusion of the goddess of love, when the reward for your fidelity is withdrawn just as you are preparing to receive it? Wouldn't it be more sensible to follow Volpone's advice and prove, "while we may, the sports of love"?[53] Better, surely, to risk gathering the rosebuds too soon than to suffer the fate of the "rathe primrose" that, in an earlier draft of the poem, died "unwedded," "colouring the pale cheek of uninjoyed love."[54]

To assume with several recent critics that Amaryllis and Neaera stand for no more than the composition of love poetry as opposed to epic poetry is, therefore, to misunderstand the whole tenor of Milton's argument. The alternative that has gradually emerged during the previous thirteen lines is not the writing of a different kind of poem; it is the living of a different kind of life. Whatever symbolic overtones the two nymphs may have acquired as a result of their association with the amatory verse of George Buchanan, the most important thing about them, as E.S. LeComte rightly reminds us, is that they are women.[55]

In particular, we may note in passing, they are the women whose presence distracts the shepherds from their pastoral labors in Virgil's Arcadia. Amaryllis makes her first appearance at the beginning of *Eclogue I*, as Meliboeus is contrasting Tityrus's good fortune with his own unhappy plight: "You Tityrus, lie under your spreading beech's covert, wooing the woodland Muse on slender reed, but we are leaving our country's bounds and sweet fields. We are outcasts from our country; you Tityrus, at ease beneath the shade, teach the woods to echo 'fair Amaryllis'" (1-5). She reappears in *Eclogue II*, when Corydon recalls how he courted her before he fell in love with the cruel Alexis. "Was it not better," he asks himself, "to brook Amaryllis' sullen rage and scornful disdain?" (14-15). Milton's allusion to her characteristically fuses the two passages into a single reference—his "meditate the thankless Muse" is clearly a variant of Virgil's "silvestrem . . . musam meditaris," while "in the shade" and "Were it not better done" translate the Latin phrases "in umbra" and "nonne fuit satius" word for word.[56] Read in this dual context, the notion of sporting with Amaryllis reverberates with ironies. Milton is proposing to abandon a thankless mistress for a nymph who was as well known for her disdain as for her beauty, and he is proposing to do so at precisely that moment in history when another group of shepherds is being deprived of its pastoral living by the tyranny of an unjust administration. Confronted by the possibility that his "laborious days" have all been wasted, Meliboeus is offering to change places with Tityrus.

This latter theme is reinforced by the association that the name of Neaera would have been likely to stir in the minds of Milton's readers. In Virgil's *Eclogue III* it is Neaera who is responsible for Aegon's refusal to take proper care of his flock: "Poor sheep, ever luckless flock! While your master courts Neaera and fears lest she prefer Menalcas to him, this hireling keeper milks his ewes twice an hour, and the flock are robbed of strength and the lambs of milk" (3-6). Long before St. Peter appears on the scene to foretell "the ruine of our corrupted Clergie," his complaints about faithless herdsmen have been anticipated by the elegist's Virgilian allusions.[57] In the very act of naming the representatives of erotic pleasure in *Lycidas*, Milton has provided himself (and us) with at least a potential reason for rejecting them.

For the time being, though, a motive so closely related to the ecclesiastical aspect of the pastoral metaphor can be no more than potential. Not until the arrival of the "Pilot of the Galilean lake" (109) will Edward King assume his role as a potential churchman. Here he is still a poet, and the immediate issue, as I have emphasized, is not the integrity of Christ's ministers but the chastity of the Muse's followers. Milton's treatment of this issue in the lines that follow owes a great deal of its power, I suspect, to the intimate connection that existed in his own mind between poetic productivity on the one hand and sexual abstinence on the other. For when the pursuit of any activity is made dependent upon the avoidance of some other, the first often turns out to be a sublimated version of the second. Alternatives, in other words, have a way of becoming substitutes. By insisting that the poetic impulse could not be fulfilled unless the erotic impulse was repressed, Milton was in effect creating an equivalence between them. Apollo takes the place of Venus, Calliope assumes the role of Amaryllis, and her devotees make poems instead of love.

It was only natural, then, that Milton should have equated the frustration of literary potentiality with the denial of sexual fulfillment. According to the correspondence worked out by Sandys and Bacon between the two kinds of propagation, to cut off the possibility of great literary works was analogous to destroying the opportunity to beget children.[58] As a result, the assault of the abhorred shears feels like a castration:

> Fame is the spur that the clear spirit doth raise
> (That last infirmity of Noble mind)
> To scorn delights, and live laborious dayes;

But the fair Guerdon when we hope to find,
And think to burst out into sudden blaze,
Comes the blind Fury with th'abhorred shears,
And slits the thin spun life. [70-76]

The barely submerged sexuality of Milton's language thus turns the pursuit of fame into an act of love.[59] But the anticipated climax never takes place. The blind fury comes instead.[60]

Phoebus Apollo's response to this crisis is generally agreed to be inadequate, either because it is couched in pagan rather than in Christian terms, or because it sounds too pat and aphoristic. The foregoing analysis suggests another and more serious reason for the failure of his admonitions to convince: they completely miss the point, which had to do not so much with losing fame as with losing the chance to earn it. By touching Milton's ear, as he had touched Virgil's in the sixth *Eclogue*, Phoebus seems to imply that the Puritan poet is getting above himself.[61] But in fact the issue here is not pride, or praise, or even fame. It is fulfillment. Confronted with the possibility that he may never be allowed to run the race for which he has spent most of his adult life training himself, what possible consolation can Milton be expected to find in the announcement that the prize-giving will be in heaven? Divine approval of the rigor of his preparations would no doubt be gratifying, but it would hardly compensate for the utter futility of undertaking them.[62] The solution simply does not address the problem, and one is left with a sense of incompleteness, of answers yet to be given.

Nevertheless, however unsuccessful the arguments themselves might be, it is particularly appropriate that the voice that expounds them should be Phoebus Apollo's. For in addition to being the god of poetry, Phoebus was also the husband of the Muse whom Milton is threatening to desert and, still more significantly, the father of the poet whose death at the hands of the Bacchantes had prompted those thoughts of desertion. "Orpheus," declared Thomas Cooper in his *Dictionarium Historicum*, was "the son (as some write) of Apollo and Calliope," and, despite Cooper's cautious parenthesis, virtually every Renaissance scholar who considered the question held the same opinion.[63] The advice Milton receives, therefore, comes from someone who has suffered a loss quite as grievous as his own, and as a result it has a special kind of authenticity. As god of poetry alone, Phoebus might be suspected of defending his own interests when he attempts to provide the poet with a reason for continuing to serve the Muse. As the bereaved father of Orpheus, on the other hand, he has more reason to share Milton's outraged feelings than to soothe them. Far from being the impersonal observations of an insensitive *deus ex machina*, Phoebus's speech implicitly exemplifies the patience it advocates.

In a transformation that is typical of the work as a whole, what at one moment appeared to be a provisional kind of ending at the next moment proves to have been the beginning of a completely new phase in the poem's development. For when we first came to Phoebus's discourse on fame, it sounded no less conclusive than the revelations of Patience in *Sonnet XIX*. As soon as Camus and the Pilot of the Galilean Lake arrive on the scene, however, we realize that the god of poetry not only brought the opening movement of the elegy to a close, but also simultaneously initiated the second movement, the procession of visitors. This radical readjustment in our perception of Phoebus's role may already have been suggested, of course, by a detail that to Milton's classically trained readers would have seemed only too obvious: Phoebus is the first of the three divinities who come to visit the dying Gallus in Virgil's tenth *Eclogue*. It may not be too fanciful, then, to hear in the god's admonitions in *Lycidas* a faint echo of his outburst in the *Eclogue:* "Gallus, what madness is this? Thy sweetheart Lycoris hath followed another amid snows and amid rugged camps" (22-23). Both the classical and the Puritan poets have been seeking fulfillment in the wrong place.

Certainly there is a close relationship between the second visitors in the two elegies. As we have seen, Milton's Camus, with his "Mantle hairy, and his Bonnet sedge, / Inwrought with figures dim, and on the edge / Like to that sanguine flower inscrib'd with woe" (104-6), bears a striking resemblance to Virgil's Silvanus.[64] The one significant characteristic that distinguishes Camus from his Virgilian predecessor is his fatherhood. While it is true, as several scholars have remarked, that rivers are often paternal (Old

Father Thames and Pater Tiber for example), I suspect that Milton may have had another reason for introducing a parent at this juncture of the poem. Given the link that I suggested earlier between *Lycidas* and *Ad Patrem*, it seems only natural that it should be Lycidas's "reverend Sire" (103) who returns to mourn the forfeiture of his "dearest pledge" (107).[65]

The relationship between the final visitors in the two poems is no less functional, for, as Milton's readers were well aware, Pan, the god of shepherds, was one of the standard types of Christ in the mythological treatises of the Middle Ages and the Renaissance.[66] Virgil describes his arrival as follows: "Pan came, Arcady's god, and we ourselves saw him, crimsoned with vermilion and blood-red elderberries. 'Will there be no end?' he cried. 'Love recks naught of this: neither is cruel Love sated with tears, nor the grass with the rills, nor bees with the clover, nor goats with leaves'" (26-30).[67] Here, perhaps, is the source of the digestive metaphor in St. Peter's speech—the sixteenth-century commentator Stephanus Riccius even substitutes sheep (*oves*) for Virgil's bees (*apes*) in his paraphrase of Virgil's text.[68] But once again the basic pattern of the original passage has been transposed. Saint Peter's point is not that the sheep are insatiable but that the shepherds are unwilling to satisfy them. What in the *Eclogue* was an illustration of the futility of grief has become in *Lycidas* a reason for succumbing to it.

The most important difference between the Pilot of the Galilean lake and his classical predecessor, however, concerns the audience rather than the content of his speech. In Virgil's *Eclogue* the visitors came to persuade the protagonist to abandon a way of life that was likely to prove fatal. In *Lycidas* the protagonist is already dead, and the visitors come not to admonish but to mourn him. It is too late for Edward King to change his mind. But it is not too late for Milton. Unlike Lycidas, the lonely shepherd who has survived to weep this "melodious tear" (14) still has time to ponder the revelations delivered by Phoebus and St. Peter. Indeed, the speech of the first visitor, as we now recognize him to have been, was specifically addressed to King's elegist. For a few moments, at least, the singer was in the position traditionally occupied by the hero of his song, and though the third visitor ostensibly directs his comments to the dead "young swain" (113) beneath the Irish Sea, it is the "uncouth Swain" (186) still living among the oaks and rills who actually hears them.

It was to St. Peter's speech, of course, that Milton was referring when he retrospectively claimed prophetic insight by adding to the headnote of the 1645 edition the famous phrase: "And by occasion foretells the ruine of our corrupted Clergy, then in their height." But if the "two-handed engine" (130) refers, as most critics now seem to agree, to St. Michael's sword in Revelation, then Milton was foretelling not simply the reform of the English church but the end of the world.[69] The sense of imminent cosmic revolution that I described in the introduction is no longer held in check, as it had been in the *Nativity Ode*: "But wisest Fate says no, / This must not yet be so" (149-50). Here the instrument of retribution is "ready" (131), and the Day of Judgement is clearly not far off. Nevertheless, the question still remains: granted that St. Michael would smite the faithless herdsmen on the last day, how is the flock to be protected in the meantime? Can ecclesiastical reform be left in abeyance merely because self-seeking ministers are destined to be punished "at the door" (130)? Shouldn't some attempt be made to remedy the current condition of the church, to banish false shepherds from the fold and hunt down the wolf in his lair?[70]

The plight of the sheep in *Lycidas* is thrown into still sharper relief by one of Milton's most significant (though least noted) departures from the pastoral tradition: his violation of the longstanding convention whereby the sheep are delegated to the care of a companion while the shepherd himself is performing the song. During the opening exchanges of Theocritus's first *Idyl*, for instance, Thyrsis accompanies his invitation to "sit down here, goatherd, on this hill slope by the tamarisks and play your pipe" with an offer to "tend your goats meanwhile" (12-14). And though Mopsus needs no persuasion to lament the death of Daphnis in Virgil's fifth *Eclogue*, Menalcas nevertheless assures him that, while he is singing, "Tityrus will tend the grazing kids" (12). For the duration of *Lycidas*, on the contrary, no one is tending the flock. Milton is warbling his Doric lay, and Edward King is dead. In the meantime, as the references to Amaryllis and Neaera have already hinted, the sheepfold has been left to the mercies of ignorant and greedy hirelings. Like the lambs in the *Epitaphium Damonis* who "go home unpastured" because their "master" is too busy singing his song to attend to them (18), the "hungry Sheep" (125) in *Lycidas* are starving for want of adequate nourishment. John Shawcross has argued that in St. Peter's condemnation of ecclesiastical corruption Milton "gives us good reason for his renunciation of the clerical life."[71] But the absence of the shepherd's traditional companion from Milton's elegy provides at least one good reason for questioning that decision. Instead of playing on his "Oaten Flute" (33), shouldn't the uncouth swain be feeding the flock himself? Were it not better done, if not to sport with Amaryllis in the shade, at least to labor for St. Peter in the sheepfold? Instead of writing poems, shouldn't John Milton be ministering to the religious needs of his fellow countrymen?

For a long time, of course, that is exactly what he had planned to do. According to the autobiographical preface to Book 2 of *The Reason of Church Government*, Milton was destined for the ministry both "by the intentions of my parents and friends" and "in mine own resolutions." But, as he goes on to explain, "perceaving what tyrany had invaded the Church," he had subsequently abandoned his plans to enter holy orders and had decided to devote himself wholly to poetry. Unfortunately, Milton does not tell us precisely when this decision took place, merely that he was "Church-outed by the Prelats" when he had arrived at "some maturity of years."[72] We cannot, therefore, be certain whether or not he still hoped to pursue an ecclesiastical career when he wrote *Lycidas*. In the unlikely event that Milton did not abandon his plans for a career in the church until the promulgation of the Constitutions and Canons Ecclesiastical in 1640, as John Spencer Hill has argued, the plight of the neglected flock must surely have exacerbated the anxiety he felt about his delay in entering the priesthood.[73] For ever since he had become eligible for ordination on his twenty-fourth birthday in 1632, Milton had been open to the charge of "belatednesse," against which he defends himself in his letter to a friend.[74] On the other hand, if we assume, as I believe we should, that Milton had abandoned his intention to enter the priesthood before he composed *Lycidas*, then the situation he describes in St. Peter's speech must surely have given him some qualms about his decision to devote himself entirely to poetry. It is true, of course, that in the *Elegia Sexta* and elsewhere he describes the poetic vocation as a kind of priesthood,[75] but here in *Lycidas* the death of Edward King has brought him face-to-face with the possibility that he had been overestimating the power of poetry. Suppose, after all, that the poet's voice was not capable of replacing the preacher's? Suppose, in W.H. Auden's words, that "poetry makes nothing happen," surviving merely "in the valley of its saying"?[76] If Orpheus's song could not allay the perturbations of the Bacchantes, what hope could Milton have of charming their seventeenth-century counterparts? Wouldn't the lean and flashy songs of false shepherds drown out his music just as surely as the hideous roar of the Maenads overwhelmed the song of Orpheus? Perhaps Milton's mouth, too, is blind. St. Peter's speech thus serves to intensify, not assuage, the anxieties implicit in the poem's title. Far from being a digression, as it is still sometimes called,[77] it touches on the central issue of Milton's entire career. In a land threatened by wolves, who will listen to the shepherd's piping?

The predicament of the hungry sheep thus drives a wedge between the two major referents of the pastoral metaphor. The life of the shepherd-poet is implicitly presented as an alternative to that of the shepherd-priest, an alternative that in the historical circumstances of 1637 may not have had very much to recommend it. "At the center of pastoral," Paul Alpers has written in an illuminating essay, "is the shepherd-singer. The great pastoral poets are directly concerned with the extent to which song that gives present pleasures can confront and, if not transform and celebrate, then accept and reconcile man to the stresses and realities of his situation."[78] In *Lycidas*, the extent to which song can accomplish these ends is problematical. Far from recording Milton's discovery of his role as a divinely inspired epic poet, as Donald Friedman has argued, Milton's elegy implicitly calls into question the efficacy of the poetic vocation itself.[79] The traditional pastoral topos of the reward for good singing has acquired a new and disturbing dimension.

In a last despairing attempt, perhaps, to test the power of

song, Milton continues with one of the most elaborately and self-consciously poetic passages in the entire poem. Like so much else in *Lycidas*, it gains significance if it is read against the background of Virgil's tenth *Eclogue*. Immediately after the speech of the final visitor, Gallus imagines an ideal landscape in which he might have disported himself, if only he had been an Arcadian shepherd: "And 0 that I had been one of you, the shepherd of a flock of yours, or the dresser of your ripened grapes! Surely, my darling, whether it were Phyllis or Amyntas, or whoever it were—and what if Amyntas be dark? Violets, too, are black and black are hyacinths—my darling would be lying at my side among the willows under the creeping vine—Phyllis culling me garlands, Amyntas singing songs. Here are cool springs, Lycoris,[80] here soft meadows, here woodland; here, with thee, time alone would wear me away" (35-43). In *Lycidas*, however, the protagonist is already dead, so in place of Edward King's voice we hear his elegist's:

> And call the Vales, and bid them hither cast
> Their Bells, and Flourets of a thousand hues.
> Ye valleys low where the milde whispers use,
> Of shades and wanton winds and gushing brooks,
> On whose fresh lap the swart Star sparely looks,
> Throw hither all your quaint enameld eyes,
> That on the green terf suck the honied showres,
> And purple all the ground with vernal flowres. . . .
> . . . .
> To strew the Laureat Herse where Lycid lies. [134-51]

The vision is still essentially pastoral, but now it is unpopulated by any living human presence. Whereas Gallus imagines himself lying in a pastoral bower beside his mistress, Lycidas lies on a laureate hearse alone. Or so Milton imagines for a moment. In fact, as he recognizes immediately afterward, the actual situation is still further removed from that in the *Eclogue*. Virgil's cool springs have given way to the "sounding Seas" (154), and King's body is lost beneath the "whelming tide" (157).[81] As a result, the attempt to interpose some pastoral "ease" (152) collapses in the face of reality; decking a drowned man with flowers, Milton realizes, is like feeding the sheep with wind. So the preceding fiction and all it stands for is dismissed as a "false surmise" (153). Poetry has attempted to perform its consolatory office, and it has failed.

Of all the reversals we have so far encountered in *Lycidas*, Milton's emphatic command to "Weep no more" (165) is easily the most violent. Without any apparent reason, the whole poem suddenly changes direction. Pagan myths give way to Christian revelation, despair turns into ecstasy, and the nightmare of a monstrous world beneath the waves is displaced by a vision of "the blest Kingdoms meek" (177) above the sky. Yet despite its abruptness, the assertion that Edward King is still alive does not take us entirely by surprise. There are several reasons for this. First, the apotheosis of the dead shepherd had been a traditional feature of the pastoral elegy since at least the time of Virgil's fifth *Eclogue*. Second, Milton had adhered in all his previous elegies to the established pattern of the Christian consolation, with its characteristic progression from mourning to rejoicing.[82] Third, and most important of all, the structural rhythm of the first two movements of the poem, each of which begins in this world and ends in the next, has already prepared us to expect an apocalyptic vision at precisely this juncture of the final movement. However inadequate it may have seemed at the time, Phoebus Apollo's discourse on fame, we now realize, prefigured the "large recompense" (184) that Edward King enjoys in the "blest Kingdoms meek."

Most readers find the Christian fulfillment considerably more satisfying than its pagan adumbration—not, I suspect, because it is better doctrine but simply because it is better poetry:

> So Lycidas sunk low, but mounted high,
> Through the dear might of him that walk'd the waves,
> Where other groves, and other streams along,
> With Nectar pure his oozy Locks he laves,
> And hears the unexpressive nuptial Song,
> In the blest Kingdoms meek of joy and love.
> There entertain him all the Saints above,
> In solemn troops, and sweet Societies

That sing, and singing in their glory move,
And wipe the tears for ever from his eyes. [172-81]

Whereas Phoebus's speech failed to offer any genuine solace for the frustration of the homely, slighted shepherd's sexual and poetic aspirations, this second account of divine reward restores the dead swain to an idealized landscape in which both impulses can be satisfied, albeit vicariously. The "blest Kingdoms meek," that is to say, are characterized by two qualities that were conspicuous by their absence in Jove's bleak court:[83] "joy and love"—joy expressed in the singing of the "sweet Societies," love in the "nuptial" union they are celebrating. For Lycidas, as the poem's original readers would have needed no reminding, is listening to the song of the hundred and forty-four thousand described in the Book of Revelation:

> And I heard the voice of harpers harping with their harps: And they sung as it were a new song before the throne, and before the four beasts, and the elders: and no man could learn that song but the hundred and forty and four thousand, which were redeemed from the earth. These are they which were not defiled with women; for they are virgins. These are they which follow the Lamb whithersoever he goeth. These were redeemed from among men. . . . And I heard as it were the voice of a great multitude, and as the voice of many thunderings, saying Alleluia! for the Lord God omnipotent reigneth. Let us be glad and rejoice, and give honour to him: for the marriage of the Lamb is come, and his wife hath made herself ready.[84]

From his late youth to his early middle age, Milton was evidently haunted by these verses—he alludes to them in the *Elegia Tertia* (1626), *At a Solemn Music* (1633), *Ad Patrem* (1637), the *Epitaphium Damonis* (1640), *The Reason of Church Government* (1642), and *Apology for Smectymnuus* (1642), as well as in *Lycidas*.[85] The reason they touched him so deeply, I believe, was not only that they described the celestial prototype of the "glorious and lofty Hymns" that he himself aspired to compose,[86] but also that they furnished scriptural authority for his faith in the sanctifying power of virginity. No one who had been "defiled with women," St. John appeared to confirm, could hope to sing the "new song" honoring the Lamb. What the Elder Brother in *Comus* called "the arms of chastity" (439) were an essential part of both the poet's and the saint's moral equipment.

At this point it may well be objected that in the *Apology for Smectymnuus* Milton took a rather different view of the matter. "Nor did I slumber," he assured his readers, "over that place expressing such high rewards of ever accompanying the Lambe, with those celestiall songs to others inapprehensible, but not to those who were not defil'd with women, which doubtlesse meanes fornication: For mariage must not be call'd a defilement."[87] But though the final reservation in favor of holy matrimony undoubtedly represents the orthodox Protestant interpretation of St. John's misogynist sentiments, there is no reason to believe that Milton adopted that interpretation until he himself was on the verge of marriage with Mary Powell in 1642.[88] On the contrary, all the evidence suggests that as late as 1640 he followed Tertullian, Jerome, and Ribera in believing that "by the undefiled [the author of the Apocalypse] understandeth such as have no wives."[89] Certainly, the conclusion of the *Epitaphium Damonis* seems to assume that the evangelist was advocating nothing less than lifelong celibacy: "Because the crimson flush of modesty and youth without stain were your pleasure, because you ne'er tasted the joys of the marriage couch, see! virginal honors are reserved for you. With your bright head encircled by a radiant crown, and carrying the gladsome shade of the bread-leaved palm, you will consummate, eternally, immortal nuptials, where there is singing, where the lyre revels madly, mingled with choirs beatific, and festal orgies run riot, in bacchante fashion, with the thyrsus of Zion" (212-19). If these lines are any indication of the way in which Milton apprehended St. John's vision when he was writing *Lycidas* just three years earlier, then the apotheosis of Edward King takes on a significant new dimension.[90] For behind the description of Damon's rapture in the *Epitaphium* lies not only the biblical account of the hymn to the Lamb, but also the neo-Platonic conception of the soul's union with God as a celestial bacchanal. "The spirit of the god Dionysius," wrote Marsilio Ficino, "was believed by the ancient theologians and Platonists to be the ecstasy and abandon of disencumbered minds, when partly by innate *love*, partly at the instigation of the god, they transgress the natural limits of intelligence and are miraculously transformed into the beloved god himself: where, inebriated by a certain new draft of *nectar* and by an immeasurable *joy*, they rage, as it were, in a bacchic frenzy."[91] In view of Milton's well-documented interest in neo-Platonic philosophy during his residence at Horton, it seems entirely plausible that the joy and love experienced by Edward King in *Lycidas* are closely related to the kind of Dionysiac ecstasy that Ficino describes in the passage above and that Damon clearly enjoys at the end of the *Epitaphium Damonis*.[92]

The most persuasive evidence in support of this hypothesis, however, is internal rather than external, for Milton's description of Lycidas among the saints is not simply a Christian fulfillment of the scene originally adumbrated by Phoebus Apollo. It is also a celestial reenactment of the events that took place still earlier in the poem on the banks of the Hebrus. The apotheosis of Lycidas, that is to say, bears a striking resemblance to the death of Orpheus at the hands of the Ciconian women. Orpheus's gory visage "down the stream was sent" (62); Lycidas washes his oozy locks "other streams along" (174). Orpheus's head was carried to "the Lesbian shore" (63); Lycidas will henceforth serve as "the Genius of the shore" (183). Orpheus was killed by "the rout that made the hideous roar" (61) because he resisted marriage; Lycidas is entertained by "solemn troops, and sweet Societies," singing a "nuptial Song" (176-79). The scene in heaven thus reads like a transcendent version (or, rather, inversion) of the scene in Thrace, harmonizing its dissonance, sublimating its violence, reviving its protagonist. In the final analysis, it is the resurrection of Lycidas rather than the intervention of Phoebus that dispels the horror of Orpheus's death.

The last eight lines of *Lycidas*, Paul Alpers has remarked, "could be the conclusion of almost any eclogue."[93] They have reminded many critics of the conclusion of Virgil's tenth *Eclogue* in particular: "These strains, Muses divine, it will be enough for your poet to have sung, while he sits idle and twines a basket of slender hibiscus. These ye shall make of highest worth in Gallus' eyes— Gallus, for whom my love grows hour by hour as fast as in the dawn of spring shoots up the green alder. Let us rise; the shade oft brings peril to singers. The juniper's shade brings peril; hurtful to the corn, too, is the shade. Get ye home, my full-fed goats—the Evening-star comes—get ye home!" (70-77). Commenting on the resemblance between this paragraph and the ending of *Lycidas*, J.H. Hanford observes that "both poems close with eight lines, very similar in spirit, referring to the end of day and the departure of the shepherd," while Merritt Hughes notes that in Milton's leave-taking we "surely hear an echo of Virgil's farewell to his Lament for Gallus."[94]

Beneath the superficial similarities between the two passages, however, there lies a radical difference that neither critic mentions: in the *Eclogue* the voice that brings the elegy to a close is the same one that began it, whereas in *Lycidas* the voice that delivers the concluding *ottava rima* belongs to a totally new speaker, one quite distinct from the shepherd who has been mourning the death of Edward King in the previous lines:

> Thus sang the uncouth Swain to th' Okes and rills,
> While the still morn went out with Sandals gray,
> He touch'd the tender stops of various Quills,
> With eager thought warbling his Dorick lay:
> And now the Sun had stretch'd out all the hills,
> And now was dropt into the Western Bay;
> At last he rose, and twitch'd his Mantle blew:
> To morrow to fresh Woods, and Pastures new. [186-93]

As Brooks and Hardy point out in their commentary, "there is no third person section at the beginning of the poem in which the 'uncouth swain' is introduced, and to which this last section recurs."[95] On the contrary, the narrator who abruptly intervenes to pronounce the swain "uncouth" is himself a completely unknown quantity.

Ever since John Crowe Ransom first drew critical attention to it in 1933, the anomalous nature of the poem's ending has been widely recognized.[96] Unfortunately, it is often discussed in terms that suggest that nothing more is involved than a last-minute switch from the present tense ("weep," "are," "wonder") to the past ("sang," "touch'd," "twitch'd"). In an attempt to refute Ransom's emphasis on Milton's idiosyncrasy, M.C. Battestin, for instance, reminds us that "authority for shifts in tense form could be found in the eclogues of Virgil."[97] So no doubt it could, but that is not the point. What cannot be found in the eclogues of Virgil, or in the eclogues of any other poet for that matter, is authority for the generic transformation that accompanies the change of tense in the final lines of *Lycidas*. For Milton's unexpected introduction of a third-person narrator at the end of a first-person poem violates one of the oldest and most fundamental covenants governing the writer's relationship with his reader: the implicit understanding that the genre of the work will remain constant, that a play will not turn into an epic halfway through, or vice versa.

The genre of *Lycidas*, the headnote informs us, is a "monody." The term derives, as Milton certainly knew, from Greek tragedy, where it means an ode sung by a single character.[98] The ensuing tribute to Edward King, we are thus led to expect, will be dramatic in character. And indeed it reads very much like a soliloquy. Up to line 185, that is to say, we seem to be in the presence of a single speaker who is addressing us in the dramatic present. But in line 186 a second, unidentified speaker suddenly emerges from the wings and with a single preterite verb thrusts the original speaker (and his speech) back into the past. A work that began as drama has ended as narrative.[99]

The general effect of this startling shift in the poem's modality is readily apparent. It is to create not only a temporal but also an ontological gap between the shepherd who sings for Lycidas and the poet who describes him doing so. The epilogue informs us, in M.H. Abrams's words, that the sentiments we have just overheard were being expressed "not by Milton but by a singer Milton is at considerable pains to identify as someone other than himself."[100] So much is obvious. The question is: why does Milton suppress this information until the poem is almost over? Or, to put it another way, why is there no matching narrative introduction to warn us in advance that the "uncouth swain" is a character in, rather than the author of, the elegy? Because, I would suggest, the distinction between the swain and Milton simply does not obtain at the beginning of *Lycidas*. Initially, at least, the two figures are identical. "In this Monody," the headnote declares, "the Author bewails a learned Friend," and there is nothing in the opening paragraphs to prevent us from taking this announcement quite literally. The voice we hear at the beginning of the poem is, unmistakably, the voice of John Milton himself, agonizing over his poetic immaturity, showing off his classical learning, recalling with evident nostalgia his days as a student in Cambridge.

As the poem progresses, however, the owner of that voice gradually loses his historical identity and finally turns into a fictional character whose values and attitudes Milton the poet does not necessarily share. The first hint that the mourner may not be a constant factor comes in line 56, when he abruptly corrects himself for reproaching the nymphs: "Ay me, I fondly dream! / Had ye bin there—for what could that have don?" Eric Smith goes rather too far, perhaps, when he comments that "the overall movement towards assurance by eliminating the misconceptions obliges us to consider the poet as in control and distinct from the speaker."[101] But the second thoughts do open up a tiny fissure in the mourner's consciousness, a fissure that widens dramatically with the intervention of the god of poetry in line 76: "But not the praise, / Phoebus repli'd, and touch'd my trembling ears." Here, as Ransom originally noted, the tense suddenly lapses from the dramatic present to the narrative past. As the experience of lines 1-75 is thrust back into an earlier time plane, a gulf opens up between the speaker who remembers Phoebus's advice and the speaker who only a few lines earlier considered abandoning his vocation. The two figures are still recognizably the same person—the ears that Phoebus touches are "my ears," not "his"—but the second figure, enlightened by the revelations of the god of poetry, speaks from a perspective considerably broader than that of his earlier manifestation.

From this point until the end of St. Peter's speech, the predominantly past tense verbs—"came" (90), "ask'd" (91), "question'd" (93), "knew" (95), "went" (103), "quoth" (107), "came," "did go" (108), "bore" (110), "shook," "bespake" (112)—

freeze the passage of time in the mourner's newly created present while he pauses to recall the speeches of the other visitors. With the invocation to Alpheus and the present imperatives that accompany it—"Return" (132), "call," "bid" (134), "Throw" (139), "purple" (141), "Bring" (142)—the clock starts running again, but almost immediately the identity of the speaker undergoes another transformation: it expands to include an undefined chorus of fellow mourners who share the speaker's "false surmise" (153) and his subsequent disillusion as he remembers the true fate of Lycidas's body. The frail thoughts and moist vows belong now to a multiple consciousness; they are "our" thoughts and vows (153, 159) rather than "mine." And a still more violent change occurs shortly afterward. At line 165, the speaker dissociates himself from his fellow mourners in a change of viewpoint so extreme that one critic has attributed what follows to a completely different character, St. Michael.[102] But we do not have to introduce an *angelus ex machina* in order to understand what is happening here. The vision of Lycidas's resurrection has detached the speaker so completely from his companions that, after addressing them directly in the second person in line 165—"Weep no more, woful Shepherds weep no more"—he is able to refer to them objectively in the third person by line 182: "Now Lycidas, the Shepherds weep no more." Spatially as well as temporally, the voice that proclaims Edward King's apotheosis is located at two removes from the voice that announced his death in the opening paragraph.

A yet more radical disjunction awaits us in line 185, however. Once again the tenses change, but, as we have already seen, the author and the genre of the poem change with them. In the last and most violent of the reversals that the poem forces us to perform, what we took for fact turns into fiction, and the swain is transformed into a figment of Milton's poetic imagination. The process of "self-objectification," as Lowry Nelson calls it, has reached its climax.[103] The entire poem, one might say, records Milton's emergence from the persona of the uncouth swain. *Lycidas* is one long act of disengagement.

Critics have reacted to this phenomenon in a variety of ways. Some, like Robert Graves, Kenneth Muir,, and E.M.W. Tillyard, ignore the concluding distinction and read *Lycidas* in purely autobiographical terms, thereby laying themselves open to the objection urged by M.H. Abrams, as noted above, that Milton clearly distinguishes himself from the swain in the final lines.[104] Others, like Barbara H. Smith, David Berkeley, and Donald M. Friedman, ignore the initial identification of the two figures and treat the swain as a dramatic persona from the very beginning. Discussing the relation of the elegist to Milton, Smith, for instance, observes, "As always, I am speaking here of the fictional person whose utterance the poem represents. And Milton himself, by introducing a framing conclusion evidently written by someone other than the 'uncouth Swain,' certainly emphasizes this fiction."[105] As I have tried to show, however, the uncouth swain does not *become* fictional until the end of the poem. At the beginning, he is the historical entity we know as John Milton. And while it is certainly legitimate to reinterpret the earlier sections of the poem retrospectively in the light of what we learn later—indeed, as we have seen, Milton's method is to force us to do so repeatedly—it is not legitimate to read the poem as if we knew from the very outset that the uncouth swain was a fictional persona. If that is how Milton intended us to respond, he would have supplied a balancing prologue. To say, with Friedman, that "Milton chose a pastoral persona" through which to speak *Lycidas* is to be wise before the event.[106]

David Berkeley has carried this view of the speaker still further in an analysis of *Lycidas* that depicts the swain as a fully fledged fictional character with whom Milton has nothing whatever in common. After reprimanding Muir for confusing "the swain as *persona* with the proper voice of the author," he characterizes the persona as "an unknowledgeable pagan" who utters "thoughts beyond his thoughts," a naive mouthpiece for religious typologies that he himself does not understand or intend.[107] Quite apart from its inherent improbability—why would a Christian scholar choose an ignorant heathen to be his spokesman in a tribute to a learned friend destined for the ministry?—this interpretation of the poem is flawed by its failure to recognize the intensely personal force of the questions Milton poses as he contemplates the implications of King's death. As Stanley Fish observes, "here is no mediated pastoral voice, heard through a screen of tradition and ritual; here is the thing itself, the expression of a distinctive perspective on a problem that others may have considered . . . but never with such poignancy and perceptiveness."[108]

At the opposite extreme from Berkeley, Clay Hunt argues in his study of *Lycidas* and the Italian critics that Milton is to be associated exclusively with the swain. It is the voice speaking the *ottava rima*, according to Hunt, that belongs to a persona. Commenting on line 185, he writes, "At this point a new speaker takes over, someone not involved with Milton's personal feelings about King's death, who looks on the scene from the outside. As he coolly describes Milton in the act of spending an entire day writing the poem, he detaches us from all personal feeling the poem has expressed."[109] The effect of the epilogue, then, in Nelson's words, is to provide "a final impression of the poem as performance," to insulate the experience it contains from any direct contact with the real world.[110]

Divergent as they are, all these readings share one fundamental assumption: the notion that "*Lycidas* is the expression of a unified consciousness."[111] From which it follows, of course, that if the swain is Milton then the voice at the end must belong to someone else, and vice versa. It seems to me, on the contrary, that *Lycidas* is the expression of a consciousness that grows increasingly divided as the poem progresses, until, at line 186, the second self becomes completely independent of the first. I cannot quite agree with Louis L. Martz, therefore, when he states that "Milton at the close reveals the presence of the mature consciousness that has guided the words of his 'uncouth swain' throughout the poem."[112] For "the mature consciousness" of the final *ottava rima* has only come into being, I believe, during the course of the elegy. It is not that the author has concealed himself behind the pastoral scenery in order to make a surprise appearance at the end. It is, rather, that the poem has acquired a new author, that Milton has undergone a transformation so profound that by the end of the poem he has become, quite literally, another person. Far from being "in control of the poem's diction from the very beginning," as Friedman asserts, the voice we hear in the *ottava rima* simply did not exist at the beginning of the poem.[113]

The conclusion of *Lycidas* thus enacts in an extraordinarily vivid way an experience analogous to, though not, I think, identical with, the Christian conversion experience. Fish describes it in terms of the disappearance of the speaker from the scene of his own poem, but there is rather more involved here than a mere disappearance.[114] For as the old speaker fades away, a new speaker is born. Like a snake sloughing its skin, the singer withdraws from his song and in the final lines begins what is essentially a new song that contains the old one. It is as if the self of a dream has suddenly awakened, like the sleeper in the *Carmina Elegiaca*, into the self of everyday reality. The elegy and the swain who sang it recede into the distance, and we are left with the sense that we have witnessed a kind of rebirth. Milton has himself undergone something like the experience he had universalized in the *Nativity Ode;* in Pauline terms, he has cast off the old man to put on the new.

But who is this new man, and what does he represent? As is so often the case with Milton's poetry, the verse form itself holds the key. The concluding eight lines of *Lycidas* are in *ottava rima*, the major vehicle of narrative poetry in the Renaissance. As Martz notes, there is, therefore, "a special decorum in this concluding metrical form," for just as Milton shifts into a "stanza that is best known for objective narration," so "the mode of the poem shifts to the third person."[115] Still more to the point, however, *ottava rima* was associated not just with narrative verse in general but with a particular kind of narrative verse. It was the standard vehicle of the sixteenth-century romantic epic, the stanza of Tasso's *Gerusalemme Liberata*, Ariosto's *Orlando Furioso*, and their English translations by Fairfax and Harington. As the verse form in which the amorous and military conquests of Roland and Godfrey had been celebrated, the *ottava rima* thus implies a great deal more than "objective narration." It invokes the turbulent world of heroic action and romantic love.[116] The concluding stanza of *Lycidas* thus carries with it a set of values diametrically opposed to those associated with the pastoral as a genre and to those associated with Edward King as a character. After the meditative, loosely organized *canzoni* preceding it, it acts like a sudden burst of adrenalin, rousing the singer from his reverie and propelling him toward the wars of truth in which "the true warfaring Christian" could show his mettle—"Arise, come, arise: now it is time . . ." The new verse form thus opens up the possibility of living an entirely different kind of life, animated no longer by the ideals of the pastoral eclogue but rather by those of the Christian epic. The course of Milton's life, it suggests, is about to undergo a drastic change.

Most critics of the poem would limit that change to the specific area of Milton's literary ambitions. While recognizing the heroic overtones of the final *ottava rima*, they take them to imply no more than a decision, analogous to Virgil's at the end of the tenth *Eclogue*, to abandon the pastoral for the epic. For John Spencer Hill, the conclusion of *Lycidas* is the prelude to "a new dawn of poetic promise," while for Wittreich it signals the entry of vision into the world of action. "His confidence in the power of song buoyed up by the story of Orpheus' success [*sic*] in liberating Eurydice," Wittreich writes, "Milton is now ready to unleash his power, his poetry, upon the world."[117] The problem, of course, is that the new day did not break for another thirty years, that for the next two decades Milton chose to unleash his power not in poetry but in prose.

If my reading of the poem is correct, on the other hand, *Lycidas* foreshadows Milton's decision to shelve his poetic ambitions. For as I have already suggested, his confidence in the power of song must have been severely shaken, if not completely subverted, by the questions that the death of Edward King had forced upon him. If songs were powerless in the face of violence and injustice, as Lycidas's namesake had been taught in the ninth *Eclogue* and as the death of Orpheus appeared to confirm, then what was the point of the self-denial that Milton believed was the prerequisite of singing them? Even the apocalyptic vision of Lycidas enjoying the rewards of abstinence in heaven could not entirely dispel the nagging fear that, in a cruel and chaotic world, it was futile to meditate the thankless muse. And if, as he was to write later in *The Reason of Church Government*, it was "folly to commit anything elaborately composed to the careless and interrupted listening of these tumultuous times," then surely he should direct his energies to some more useful activity.[118] What is more, as I have argued, the abuses identified in St. Peter's speech cried out so desperately for reform that any further prolongation of his pastoral retreat had become unthinkable. It was time to lose his political as well as his sexual virginity, "to leave a calm and pleasing solitariness, fed with cheerful and confident thought, to embark in a troubled sea of noises and hoarse disputes."[119] The moral of *Lycidas* is almost the opposite of Voltaire's in *Candide:* "Il faut quitter notre jardin." "To morrow to fresh woods and pastures new."[120]

That much misquoted final line is deceptively simple. After the past tenses of the other verbs in the stanza, it suddenly reverts back into a vague kind of present: "To morrow to . . ." What the grammar does not make clear, however, is just who is planning to set off. Is it the uncouth swain or John Milton? The answer, I would suggest, is both, for despite the disjunction we have analyzed the uncouth swain is still a part of Milton. We cannot leave our pasts behind us like a landscape; what we have been is still part of what we are. So, in the final line of the poem, the swain's voice merges with his author's in a declaration that means something different for each of them. In the swain's mouth, it affirms his will to go on, his determination to persist in the homely slighted shepherd's trade despite the death of his friend. By accepting the possible futility of his labors and pursuing them regardless, the swain finally offers a concrete response to the anguished questions he had posed earlier in his song. Even if it "boots" nothing to meditate the thankless muse, he will still continue to serve her. Just as Lycidas himself has risen from his watery grave, so the swain now seems to undergo a kind of resurrection—"At last he rose"—and we are left with the vision of a man, reinvigorated and reassured, setting out to face whatever the world has in store for him, much like Adam and Eve at the end of *Paradise Lost.* As John Shawcross has put it, *Lycidas* is "a farewell to the past, a heralding of the future."[121]

In Milton's mouth, on the other hand, the final line announces his departure from the pastoral world and all it stands for. At last he has broken out of the sterile, repetitive cycle in which he was trapped in the opening lines. "Yet once more" has given way to "no more" and finally to "fresh woods and pastures new." Whereas in *Ad Patrem* he had declared, "no more shall I mingle, a figure obscure, with the witless populace, but my footsteps will avoid eyes profane" (103-4), now he writes to Charles Diodati: "What am I doing? Growing my wings and meditating flight; but as yet our Pegasus raises himself on very tender pinions."[122] The bird is about to leave the nest.[123] Milton has not only described the Miltonic moment; he has lived it.

Like Marvell's *Horatian Ode*, then, *Lycidas* is about an epiphany. No longer content to sing his "numbers languishing" in the shades of Horton, Milton is about to abandon that part of himself represented by the swain, with his devotion to chastity, retirement, and poetry, in order to pursue the open-ended future of heroic and erotic engagement that the verse form has invoked. Five years later, at all events, he was doing precisely what Boccaccio and the commentators on Theocritus and Virgil had insisted a poet should not be doing: embroiling himself in the dust and heat of politics and marriage. Despite the ringing declarations of poetic ambition in Book 2 of *The Reason of Church Government*, despite the dramatic drafts in the Trinity Manuscript, the fact is that the world had to wait three decades for the appearance of *Paradise Lost*. Not until the dying days of the Commonwealth, when he was almost sixty, would Milton reassume that part of his identity which he had discarded at the end of *Lycidas* and take up the mantle of the shepherd poet yet once more.

Conclusion

THE POETICS OF
REDEMPTION

> In all human societies, the great majority of ceremo-
> nial occasions are 'rites of transition.' . . . In general
> these initial rites of separation have the effect of re-
> moving the initiate from normal existence; he (she)
> becomes temporarily an abnormal person existing in
> abnormal time. . . . Following the 'rite of separation'
> there follows an interval of social timelessness. . . . The
> general characteristic of such rites of marginality (*rites
> de marge*) is that the initiate is kept physically apart from
> ordinary people, either by being sent away from the
> normal home surroundings altogether or by being tem-
> porarily housed in an enclosed space from which ordi-
> nary people are excluded. . . . Finally, in the third phase,
> the initiate is brought back into normal society and
> aggregated to his (her) new role.
>
> —Edmund Leach,
> *Culture and Communication*, 35, 77-78

MORE THAN THIRTY YEARS after the composition of *Lycidas*, when
the fresh woods and pastures new had become a barren wilderness
of shattered hopes and failed ambitions, Milton returned once again
to the central issue that had animated his elegy for Edward King:
the nature of the virtuous life. He had already produced in *Para-
dise Lost* a devastating critique of misdirected revolutionary activ-

ism. To counterbalance that portrayal of false heroism, he now felt compelled to offer one or more positive models of virtuous conduct. He based them, I want to suggest in conclusion, on the very same ideas and principles that had informed his earlier poems. Both *Paradise Regained* and *Samson Agonistes* recapitulate in their different ways the ethical and literary vision implicit in the Miltonic moment.

To begin with, both these later works are fundamentally "rites of transition," in Edmund Leach's phrase. Christ's temptation by Satan, for example, represents a pivotal moment in his own experience as a man: the moment when he becomes the Messiah. Up to the point at which *Paradise Regained* begins, that is to say, Christ's life has been "Private, unactive, calm, contemplative" (2.82); he has been living quietly with his parents, "obscure / Unmarkt, unknown" (1.24-25), in Nazareth. From the point at which the poem concludes, his life will be public, active, mobile, dynamic; he will soon embark upon the revolutionary ministry that will eventually lead him to Calvary. The contrast in *Samson Agonistes* is even starker. Before the opening scene, Samson has been toiling "at the Mill with slaves / Himself in bonds under Philistian yoke" (41-42); having failed to liberate his people from their captivity, he has been blinded, humiliated, and imprisoned by "Israel's oppressors" (233). At the end of the play he will finally fulfill the role of Israel's deliverer, triumphing over the idolatrous Philistines with a feat of superhuman strength that will annihilate the "choice nobility and flower" (1654) of his former captors. Once again Milton has chosen to explore the "decisive instant" in each story, the fulcrum around which the protagonist's biography turns.

Like the *Nativity Ode*, *Comus*, and *Lycidas*, too, both *Paradise Regained* and *Samson Agonistes* seem to take place in a discrete narrative space, a zone of temporal and geographical intermediacy lying outside the chronological flow of everyday events. Like the dark wood in *Comus*, the "Desert wild" where Christ is tempted is "far from track of men" (1.191-93), "by humane steps untrod" (298), and his absence is perceived by his mother and the disciples as a hiatus, a mysterious interruption in the Messianic narrative, during which all they can do is wait for their redeemer to reenter the historical process. By the same token, the "unfrequented place"

(17) in which the action of *Samson Agonistes* takes place is far removed from the "popular noise" (16) of daily life in Gaza, and Samson receives his various visitors there while he enjoys a brief respite from his "servile toil" (5), on a Philistine feast-day when "Laborious works" (14) are forbidden. The action of the play is quite literally a "vacation exercise," "an interval of social timelessness" in which, as Leach puts it, the protagonist "is kept physically apart from ordinary people."

Finally, Milton's last two poems also resemble his earlier ones in their common focus on privation. Christ's principal task in *Paradise Regained* is not to undertake any positive action, but simply to reject the various courses of action proposed by his adversary, while in *Samson Agonistes* the protagonist not only spends most of his time on stage refusing the offers made to him by his father and his wife, but also achieves his final goal by an act of apocalyptic destruction comparable to the eradication of "leprous sin" and "Hell itself" (138-39) in the *Nativity Ode*. In both cases all of the emphasis is on the rejection or eradication of wickedness rather than on the active performance of virtuous deeds; once again, good is conceived in essentially negative terms, as an absence of evil.

In at least one respect, however, *Paradise Regained* and *Samson Agonistes* take us a step beyond their predecessors: they offer a coherent rationale for what might otherwise appear to be a purely idiosyncratic decision on Milton's part to focus on the prologue to action rather than on the action itself. For the first time, the Miltonic moment is situated within a conceptual structure that allows us to understand why the poet chose to write about the scene at the manger *before* the wise men and shepherds arrived, about the events that *preceded* the Egerton children's arrival at Ludlow Castle, about the *prelude* to the poet's rebirth at the end of *Lycidas*. In *Paradise Regained*, as we shall see, that structure is primarily theological; in *Samson Agonistes* it is primarily psychological. But in both cases it reveals the underlying significance of Milton's lifelong preoccupation with the decisive instants that prepare the way for fresh beginnings.

As Robert Thyer once remarked, perhaps the single most remarkable thing about Milton's brief epic is its subject.[1] The title might lead a reader coming to it for the first time to expect an account of the Passion, but Milton insists that paradise was regained not in the garden of Gethsemane or on the hill of Calvary but in the Galilean wilderness. The explanation for his decision to make Christ's temptation the subject of the poem is to be found, I believe, in Milton's distinctive doctrine of the redemption. Ever since the ode, *Upon the Circumcision*, Milton had conceived of our salvation as an essentially two-stage process. During the first stage, the son of God "Intirely satisfi'd" that "great Cov'nant which we still transgress" (21-22); that is to say, he annulled the Fall by obeying the law that Adam had broken. During the second stage, he bore on our behalf "the full wrath beside / Of vengeful Justice" (23-24); he annulled the consequences of the Fall by paying the penalty that Adam had incurred.

The same fundamental distinction between Christ's obedience, on the one hand, and his self-sacrifice, on the other, lies at the heart of Milton's analysis of "the ministry of redemption" in *De Doctrina*. "The satisfaction of Christ," he wrote, "is the complete reparation made by him in his twofold capacity of God and man, by the fulfilment of the law, and payment of the required price for all mankind."[2] Once again, the satisfaction of the covenant that Adam violated must precede the satisfaction of divine justice on the cross. Thus, when Michael tells Adam how his sin will be undone, in Book 12 of *Paradise Lost*, he divides the process into two clearly differentiated phases. Christ will begin by "fulfilling that which thou didst want, / Obedience to the Law of God, impos'd / On penaltie of death" (12.396-98). Then he will complete his redemptive mission by "suffering death, / The penaltie to thy transgression due, / And due to theirs which out of thine will grow: / So onely can high Justice rest appaid" (12.398-401). Not until Adam's disobedience has been neutralized by Christ's "patience" in the face of Satan's temptations in the wilderness can the "heroic martyrdom" of Calvary proceed.[3]

Of these two components in the redemptive process, the second is clearly an inimitable act of divine love. "It is in vain," Milton remarked in *De Doctrina*, "that the evidence of these texts is endeavored to be evaded by those who maintain that Christ died, not in our stead, and for our redemption, but merely for our advantage in the abstract, and as an example to mankind."[4] Like Sir Philip Sidney before him, however, Milton believed that the principal function of literature was to offer the reader exemplary patterns of virtuous behavior upon which his or her own conduct could be modeled. It was only natural, therefore, that he should select as the subject of *Paradise Regained* the one episode in the history of our salvation that a devout reader could reasonably aspire to imitate: Christ's "obedience to the Law of God" in the wilderness.

This decision has often been interpreted as a reflection of Milton's alleged predilection for the contemplative rather than the active life. According to Merritt Y. Hughes, for example, Christ's renunciation of worldly glory and physical pleasure signals a return to the ideals of medieval monasticism.[5] But as Milton makes clear not only in the passages I have already quoted but also in the body of *Paradise Regained* itself, the intellectual encounter with Satan is only the prelude to the public ministry and the martyrdom that are to follow. "What if he hath decreed that I shall *first* / Be try'd in humble state," Christ asks his tempter,

> Suffering, abstaining, quietly expecting
> Without distrust or doubt, that he may know
> What I can suffer, how obey? who best
> Can suffer, best can do; best reign, who *first*
> Well hath obey'd. [3.188-96, my emphasis]

The contemplative life of self-denial and obedience is not an alternative to the active life of redemptive love; it is merely the necessary first stage of a process that also involves doing and reigning. Milton is not advocating a retreat to the chaste pastoral landscape of *Lycidas;* he is simply insisting that it is the best training ground for active service in the everyday world.

Other, more recent critics have been less concerned with the reasons for Milton's choice of subject than with its consequences. The Christ of *Paradise Regained*, they complain, is a profoundly unsympathetic figure, a frigid and querulous naysayer far removed from the compassionate Jesus of the rest of the Gospel narrative.[6] Undeniably, there is more than a hint of the Puritan ascetic in

Milton's portrayal of the savior, but given the logic of the redemptive process described in *Paradise Lost* and *De Doctrina* it is hard to see how the poet could have avoided the relentless negativity of Christ's response to the devil's temptations. Since Adam's original sin had been a sin of *commission*, the performance of a forbidden act, it could only be canceled out by a virtue of *omission*, the nonperformance of a forbidden act. As a result, Christ's obedience inevitably takes the form of rejecting wicked courses of action rather than that of undertaking good ones. As a moral exemplar, the protagonist of *Paradise Regained* thus displays precisely the same kind of virtue as that demonstrated by Lady Alice Egerton in Ludlow wood: the virtue of privation. In Northrop Frye's words, both Christ and the Lady "are either motionless or unmoved and have only the ungracious dramatic function of saying No."[7]

In the later poem, however, this general impression is continuously qualified by Milton's insistence that, after saying "No" to Satan, Christ will say "Yes" to the Father. Over and over again we are reminded that the temptation in the wilderness is only the beginning of Christ's redemptive mission. Early in Book 1, for example, the Father tells Gabriel that, though the son is eventually destined to drive the devil back to hell,

> *first* I mean
> To exercise him in the Wilderness,
> There he shall *first* lay down the rudiments
> Of his great warfare, e're I send him forth
> To conquer Sin and Death . . . [1.155-59, my emphasis]

And at the end of the poem the angelic choir confirms the Father's definition of the temptation as a preliminary to the main event. Now that Christ has "regain'd lost Paradise" by "vanquishing / Temptation" (4.607-8), they exhort him to proceed to the next step: "on thy glorious work / Now enter, and begin to save mankind" (4.634-35). Although the final lines return Christ to his mother's house, Milton has made it clear that the "Queller of Satan" (4.634) is only on the brink of his divine mission. The real action is just about to begin.

The implications of this bipartite theory of the redemption

illuminate Milton's entire poetic career. For if the rejection of evil—the strategy of exclusion, as I called it in chapter 1—is the necessary prelude to the performance of good, if the slate must be wiped clean before the story of our salvation can be written on it, then Milton's consistent focus on the "decisive instant" immediately preceding moral action begins to make theological sense. Just as the death of the old man makes possible the birth of the new in the *Nativity Ode*, just as the virtue of omission prepares the way for the virtue of commission in *Comus*, just as a life of retirement and chastity proves to be the prelude to a life of political and erotic engagement in *Lycidas*, so Christ's refusal to succumb to Satan's temptations earns him the right to conquer his adversary at Calvary. Before evil has been rejected, before the pagan gods have been expelled or the evil tempter repulsed, fallen nature is scarcely a fit subject for poetry. Yet when the process of rejection has been completed, when the lost paradise has been reclaimed and the soul has been purified, then the time has come for virtuous deeds rather than poetic reflection. So what Milton writes about is almost invariably the crucial interim between the two conditions, the psychological and spiritual gap between the state of sin and the state of grace. The Miltonic moment is ultimately a moment of purification, of catharsis, without which the moral victory of good would be impossible. In the final analysis, Milton's "choice of moments" reflects his profound conviction that the old man must die before the new man can be reborn.

If *Paradise Regained* provides the clearest statement of the theological and moral rationale for the Miltonic moment, *Samson Agonistes* offers the poet's most profound and moving account of its psychological ramifications. To begin with, the retrospect here is neither authorial, as in *Lycidas* and *Paradise Regained*, nor narratorial, as in the *Nativity Ode* and *Comus*, but strictly personal:

> O wherefore was my birth from Heaven foretold
> Twice by an Angel? . . .
> Why was my breeding order'd and prescrib'd
> As of a person separate to God
> Designed for great exploits; . . .

> . . . Promise was that I
> Should Israel from Philistian yoke deliver . . . [23-39]

The past that is being remembered is the speaker's own. Nor is the act of looking backward confined to Samson's opening speech. Throughout the rest of the play Israel's would-be deliverer is haunted by the memory of "Times past," tormented by the contrast between "what once I was, and what am now" (22). Indeed, the dialogue consists very largely of extended flashbacks as Samson and his various visitors recall the highlights of his earlier career. In his dictionary, *The New World of English Words*, Milton's nephew, Edward Phillips, interpreted the name Samson to mean "there for the second time." His gloss accurately defines the essence of Samson's experience in the play. As he analyzes his personal history with Manoa, Dalila, Harapha, and the chorus, Samson seems to be living his life all over again.

What is more, as John Guillory has pointed out, many of the most important episodes in the story literally happen twice.[8] Samson's birth is "foretold / Twice by an Angel" (23-24); he marries twice; he is betrayed by his wife twice; the officer comes twice to order him to attend the feast of Dagon; and he receives divine instructions to violate the Nazarite law twice. The repetitions are almost as insistent as they were in *Lycidas* and just as significant, for on each occasion the second occurrence precipitates an outcome entirely different from that of the first. Nothing happens after the original angelic prophecy; after the second, Samson is born. Samson's first marriage fails to bring about "Israel's Deliverance" (225); the second eventually leads to his victory over the Philistines. In response to the officer's initial demand, Samson refuses to accompany him to the temple; when the officer returns, Samson complies. The "Divine impulsion" (422) to marry a Philistine woman brought disaster in its wake; the "rouzing motions" (1382) that direct him to the feast of Dagon make possible his final victory. Just as the recurrences in *Lycidas* frequently corrected their antecedents, just as Christ's rejection of the devil's temptations in *Paradise Regained* canceled out Adam's surrender to them in *Paradise Lost*, so here Samson's second chances enable him to redeem his prior failures. Once again, recollection is of the essence.

So powerful is the retrospective impulse in this text, indeed, that it has seemed to many readers, beginning with Dr. Johnson, that the play's center has been drained of all dramatic energy, that Milton's tragedy "must be allowed to want a middle."[9] Not surprisingly, therefore, the critical history of *Samson Agonistes* consists very largely in the efforts of its admirers to discover (or manufacture) a dramatic action that will fill the apparent void between the opening scene and the final catastrophe. By far the most popular line of argument has been the so-called "regenerist" reading of the play, elaborated by Arthur E. Barker, Ann Gossman, W.R. Parker, J.M. Steadman, and A.S.P. Woodhouse, among others.[10] The "middle" of *Samson Agonistes*, according to these critics, consists of "a gradual process of regeneration during the course of which Samson, through the trials or temptations brought about by his visitors, changes from a man of despair to a champion of God."[11] Far from being a disconnected series of debates that serve, as Johnson put it, neither to "hasten nor retard the catastrophe," the hero's encounters with his visitors are a progressive series of temptations analogous to those experienced by Christ in *Paradise Regained*. By resisting them, the regenerist critics conclude, Samson eventually achieves the grace that enables him to fulfill his divine mission. In Gossman's words, "Temptation is the means of causing Samson to assert and manifest his virtue and intelligence and thereby to be regenerated. . . . Through the visits of Manoa, Dalila, and Harapha, Samson is tried and purified, made ready for his last triumphant ordeal." After his moral victories over his father's skepticism, his wife's sexual allurements, and the giant's insults, "Samson now needs only an opportunity to display his newly won strength and virtue."[12]

There are several serious problems with this interpretation of the play, not least of which is the fact that the options presented by Manoa and Dalila do not seem to be intrinsically wicked, while Harapha does not propose any course of action at all. In order to characterize Manoa and Dalila as tempters, regenerist critics are consequently forced to misrepresent the purpose of their visits. John Spencer Hill, for instance, offers the following summary of Samson's encounter with his father: "Manoa presumes that Samson's mission is over and that God has no further need of him—and he asks his son to act on this assumption."[13] Yet Milton's text makes it perfectly clear that Manoa presumes nothing of the kind. On the contrary, he points out that if God had no further use for Samson he would never have restored his "strength Miraculous" (588). "His might continues in thee not for naught," he tells his son, "Nor shall his wondrous gifts be frustrate thus" (589-90). If this exhortation to faith in God's omnipotence is a temptation, then it is a temptation to which Samson would do well to succumb.

The same might be said of Dalila's plea for forgiveness. For as William Empson enquired a quarter of a century ago, if it was right for Adam to pardon the wife who betrayed him, why is it wrong for Samson to do the same thing?[14] Moreover, what sinister reason could Dalila possibly have for seeking his forgiveness? What possible motive other than "conjugal affection" (739) could prompt her to offer to care for her blind husband for the rest of his life? As Irene Samuel has observed, "tending that wrecked hulk of a man would hardly be the dream of a sensual enchantress or deliberate villainess."[15] Virginia Mollenkot is surely right when she asserts that critics who join Samson in crying "hyena" must "carry the burden of explaining some other plausible motivation" than marital love.[16]

A still more fundamental objection to the regenerist reading arises as soon as we consider its theological implications. For the notion that Samson "is allowed to *earn* this spiritual ransom or redemption" by his own efforts, that he has "made himself 'his own Deliverer,'"[17] would surely have scandalized any right-minded Protestant living in the seventeenth century. Christ might be able to earn the right to save mankind in *Paradise Regained*, but as a fallen human being Samson can do no more than cooperate with divine grace if and when it is given. The notion that Samson's works could possibly merit the reward of divine grace would have been anathema not only to Milton but to the overwhelming majority of his readers. Only if Samson were taken to be a typological foreshadowing of Christ, as Krouse once argued, could the underlying Pelagianism of the regenerist argument be effectively sanitized.[18]

The regenerist reading was vigorously challenged not long

after it appeared, however, by G.A. Wilkes and Irene Samuel, in two groundbreaking articles, and again several years later by J.A. Wittreich, in a book-length study of the play.[19] Unfortunately, even though I believe Wittreich is correct in arguing that the received reading of the play as a drama of redemption patterned on Christ's victory over Satan is without textual or historical warrant, the reading that he proposes in its place has even less to recommend it. According to Wittreich, "Milton's poem is not about Samson's regeneration but, instead, about his second fall," and the work as a whole is "less a celebration than a censure of its hero."[20] Samson, he argues, was tragically mistaken in his belief that God could suspend his own laws by instructing him to marry Philistine women or to attend the festivities of Dagon; the chorus's defense of Samson's marriage in lines 300-325 is dismissed as "pernicious casuistry" (69). Lust and vengefulness rather than divine impulsion prompted these violations of the Nazarite law, from which it follows that the destruction of the temple was a barbarous perversion of Samson's divine mission. Manoa is quite wrong, therefore, when he asserts that Samson acted "With God not parted from him, as was fear'd / But favoring and assisting to the end" (1719-20), and his assurance that "Nothing is here for tears, . . . nothing but well and fair, / And what may quiet us in a death so noble" (1721-24) is pure self-delusion. The final choric ode proclaiming "calm of mind, all passion spent" (1758) offers no more than "a false equilibrium" (221). If Wittreich is to be believed, then, *Samson Agonistes* is "a symbolic inversion, a counter-commentary" on *Paradise Regained* (131). Against the true heroism of Christ in the wilderness, Milton has set the false and destructive heroism of Samson in the temple.

The fundamental implausibility of this reading may be gauged by considering Milton's reference to the Samson story in a passage Wittreich cites from the *First Defense*. Samson, Milton writes, "whether instigated by God or by his own valor only, slew not one but many of his country's tyrants. And as he had first duly prayed to God to be his help, it follows that he counted it not wickedness, but a duty to kill his masters, his country's tyrants, even though the greater part of his countrymen refused not slavery."[21] Wittreich interprets this to mean that Samson's motives for slaughtering the

Philistines are being called into question. The context of the passage makes it unambiguously clear, however, that Milton wholeheartedly agreed with Samson that it was "not wickedness, but a duty," to kill "his country's tyrants," for the whole point of the allusion is to justify Parliament's execution of Charles I. As he reveals in his preceding example of Ehud, who slew Eglon, the king of Moab, Milton regarded the elimination of tyrants as a self-evident good that automatically implied divine approval: "To be sure, Ehud, who slew [Eglon] is believed to have had a warrant from God for so doing. What greater argument of its being a warrantable and praiseworthy action? God uses not to put men upon deeds that are unjust, treacherous, and cruel, but upon deeds honorable and praiseworthy. . . . If Ehud killed him justly, we too have done justly in putting Charles to death."[22]

The truth is that Milton and his revolutionary contemporaries were rather less scrupulous about destroying their enemies than a peaceable, humane, and tolerant academic living in the aftermath of Belsen and Hiroshima is likely to be. Believing as he does that the informing spirit of all Milton's writings is "their abiding humanity," Wittreich finds it inconceivable that the author of *Samson Agonistes* could have intended us to rejoice with Manoa and the chorus over the wholesale destruction of his nation's adversaries. Yet however offensive the slaughter of the Philistines might be to our modern sensibilities, we should not allow our moral revulsion to blind us to the fact that the man who applauded Cromwell's massacres in Ireland would have been unlikely to lose any sleep over Samson's vengeance on "his country's tyrants."

If neither the regenerist nor the humanitarian reading of *Samson Agonistes* is altogether satisfactory, then, how can the play be defended against Johnson's strictures? How is the middle of *Samson Agonistes* related to its beginning and its end? We may find the starting point for an answer in my earlier definition of the Miltonic moment as the interval "between an end and a beginning."[23] As such, it is the exact opposite of the Aristotelian definition of a dramatic "middle" as the connecting link between a beginning and an end: "A beginning is that which does not itself follow anything by causal necessity, but after which something naturally is or comes to be. An end, on the contrary, is that which itself naturally follows some other thing, either by necessity, or as a rule, but has nothing following it. A middle is that which follows something [by causal necessity] as some other thing follows it [either by necessity, or as a rule]."[24] The basis of this definition, of course, is the "law of probability or necessity," as Aristotle called it, the law that in his view constituted both the unifying principle of the physical universe and the indispensable essence of a dramatic plot. The whole point of Milton's drama, on the contrary, is that human history is governed not by the laws of nature but by the eternal providence of God. *Samson Agonistes* was composed "after the antient manner" of Greek tragedy for precisely the same reason that the *Nativity Ode* was modeled on Virgil's fourth *Eclogue*, *Comus* was modeled on the court masque, *Lycidas* was modeled on the pastoral elegy, and *Paradise Lost* was modeled on the classical epic: to challenge and subvert the ideology of its generic prototype. Just as the *Nativity Ode* rewrites the return of the Golden Age, just as *Comus* reforms the cult of neo-Platonic love, just as *Lycidas* interrogates the value of chastity and retirement, just as *Paradise Lost* offers a revolutionary new definition of heroic virtue, so *Samson Agonistes* confutes the fundamental principle of classical tragedy as Aristotle had defined it. The events of Milton's play are unified not by the law of probability or necessity but, in Wilkes's words, by "the sovereignty of providence, undistracted by man's errors and deserts, moving invincibly toward the objective proposed."[25]

It seems to me, therefore, that the *dis*connection between Samson's initial dilemma and his ultimate victory, far from being a dramatic flaw, is absolutely critical to Milton's meaning. The first phase of Samson's history is over when we first meet him; his attempts to liberate his people have ended in failure and betrayal. The second phase, which will culminate in the destruction of the temple, is just starting as he leaves the stage with the officer. Between them there stretches neither an interlinked chain of cause and effect of the kind that Aristotle envisioned, nor a gradual ascent from despair to redemption of the kind that regenerist critics have posited, but a prolonged moment of hiatus, a period of psychological and spiritual suspension, at the end of which the direction of Samson's life will be utterly transformed. Up to the moment at which Samson experiences his "rouzing motions," the play is an extended intermission between the first and last acts of his personal drama.

During its course, Samson resembles no one so much as the Adam of Book 10 of *Paradise Lost*, trapped in the sterile solitude of "the Hell within him" (4.20). In Adam's case, too, several critics have suggested that, during the course of his great soliloquy that begins in line 720, the protagonist succeeds in groping his way out of his inner darkness. But if there is any such development it is hard to detect, for Adam's speech does not really progress at all. It consists, rather, of a series of false starts that keep circling back "with dreadful revolution" (814) to the point of departure, the guilty self at the center:

> all my evasions vain,
> And reasonings, though through Mazes, lead me still
> But to my own conviction: first and last
> On mee, mee onely, as the sourse and spring
> Of all corruption, all the blame lights due. [829-33]

Every path Adam tries turns out to be a cul-de-sac; over and over again he is forced to retrace his steps and start afresh. His insistent questions—almost half the speech is in the interrogative—twist and turn in desperation, but each "yet" and "but"—nine sentences begin with one or the other—signals another dead end. The whole frustrating process is reenacted grammatically by Adam's habit of making himself the object of his own verbs; his speech is so reflexive that it contains as many me's as I's. Even the syntax is a vicious circle. Like the characters in Sartre's *No Exit*, the hero of *Paradise Lost* is engaged in a hopeless search for the way out of a hell without doors.

In much the same way, Samson's thoughts and feelings reproduce the circular motion of his labor at the mill. Just as he pushes the grindstone around and around, so his thoughts revolve and revolve, always returning to the same point of departure. In his first speech, for instance, he recognizes quite clearly that he is responsible for what has happened to him: "what if all foretold / Had been fulfill'd but through mine own default? / Whom have I to complain of but myself?" (44-46). In response to the chorus's first words to him he makes exactly the same point:

> How could I once look up, or heave the head,
> Who like a foolish Pilot have shipwreck't
> My Vessel trusted to me from above,
> Gloriously rigg'd. [197-200]

During his conversation with Manoa he assures his father that, "Nothing of these evils hath befall'n me / But justly; I myself have brought them on, / Sole Author I, sole cause" (374-76). In reply to Dalila's reproaches he acknowledges, "I to myself was false ere thou to me" (824). And at the beginning of his confrontation with Harapha he admits that "these evils I deserve and more, / Acknowledge them from God inflicted on me / Justly" (1169-71). Over and over again he returns, like Adam, to "[his] own conviction." There is no detectable progression here, no moral or spiritual development, only the "dreadful revolution" of a mind circling endlessly around its own guilt. Small wonder that his moment of deepest despair and self-loathing comes, as Wilkes and Mason Tung have noted,[26] on the heels of Harapha's departure, the very moment at which the regenerist theory would lead us to expect a fervent declaration of spiritual renewal: "But come what will, my deadliest foe will prove / My speediest friend, by death to rid me hence, / The worst that he can give, to me the best" (1262-64).

Then, suddenly, unexpectedly, undeservedly, he experiences the "rouzing motions" (1382) that will lead him to his triumphant act of destruction in the temple. This is a *deus ex machina* with a vengeance, for nothing that has happened in the play so far serves to bring about God's intervention at precisely this point of the action—nothing Samson has done or said or felt has merited the internal illumination that allows him to realize that God wants him to obey the officer's instructions after all. This is not to say, however, that Samson plays no role whatsoever in his own rehabilitation. Wilkes goes too far, I think, when at the end of an otherwise persuasive rebuttal of the regenerist theory he argues that God's instructions effectively "overrule" Samson's own will, that divine providence operates "independent[ly] of Samson's volition," and that Samson "is powerless to impede [it]."[27] This makes Milton sound like an orthodox Calvinist preoccupied with the idea of divine omnipotence rather than that of human freedom. But in fact Milton did not believe in the Calvinist doctrine of irresistible grace. Like the Arminian that he had become by the time he wrote *Paradise Lost*, he believed that God's "Prevenient Grace" (11.3) had restored to every descendant of Adam and Eve the ability to exercise their free will.[28] Samson could *choose* whether or not to cooperate with divine grace; he could have ignored or disobeyed the divinely inspired "motions" of his spirit. His heroism consists not in his rejection of the proposals presented by his visitors, as the regenerist theory implies, but in his acceptance of God's "intimate impulse" (223) even though it had led to defeat and humiliation in the past. God may have been "favouring and assisting to the end" (1720), as Manoa insists, but Samson's victory over the Philistines was ultimately the product of his own freely made decision.

What distinguishes *Samson Agonistes* from all of Milton's other works, of course, is that the culminating event, far from being projected into a future that lies beyond the limits of the text itself, actually takes place within it. Even though it occurs offstage and has to be reported by a messenger, the dénouement is contained within the dramatic framework. If the play conformed to the pattern of the other works we have examined, it would end at line 1440 with the chorus's optimistic reflections on Samson's departure for the temple, not with his triumphant death. For this reason, if for no other, *Samson Agonistes* reads like an unmistakably terminal work, for the inclusion of the anticipated climax within the structure of the play provides an emphatic punctuation point to Milton's literary and political career. Here at last is the sense of closure, the decisive action, that was only foreshadowed in the final lines of all his previous poems. No longer is the world all before us as we reach the conclusion of *Samson Agonistes*; the restless "passion" that had looked forward to fresh woods and pastures new at the end of virtually every poem Milton ever wrote is finally "spent" (1758).

NOTES

Note: For full bibliographical information see the accompanying bibliography on pages 153-65.

INTRODUCTION

1. Ruskin, "Mornings in Florence," 248-54.

2. P. Toesca, *Giotto*, quoted in Martindale and Baccheschi, *Complete Paintings of Giotto*, 14.

3. Kerrigan, *The Prophetic Milton*, 228.

4. In the prose theme on early rising the emphasis on the various senses is even more obvious: "Would you delight your eyes? Look at the sun rising in ruddy vigor. . . . Would you delight your ears? Listen to the clear concert of the birds and the light humming of the bees. Would you please your nostrils? You cannot have enough of the sweetness of the scents that breathe from the flowers" (*CW,* 12:289). Milton mentions only sight, hearing, and smell, presumably, because these are the first senses to be activated. Touch and taste are likely to be engaged only when the sleeper is fully awake.

5. Kerrigan, *The Prophetic Milton*, 228.

6. Parker, *Inescapable Romance*, chapter 3.

7. Wilding, *Dragons Teeth*; Norbrook, "Milton's Early Poetry," in his *Poetry and Politics.*

8. Hill, *Experience of Defeat*; Loewenstein, *Milton and the Drama of History*; Norbrook, *Poetry and Politics.*

9. Francis Rous, *The Diseases of Time* (London, 1622), quoted in Patrides and Wittreich, eds., *Apocalypse*, 222. On Napier see Christianson, *Reformers and Babylon*, 97-98.

10. See Loewenstein, *Milton and the Drama of History*, 10-12.

11. Brightman, *A Revelation of the Revelation* (1609), quoted in Loewenstein, *Milton and the Drama of History*, 11.

12. Milton, *Animadversions Upon the Remonstrants Defence* (*CW,* 3:148).

13. My definition of the Miltonic moment, consequently, has

something in common with Catherine Belsey's notion that Milton's poetry records a series of turning points either in "the relations between heaven and earth" or in the transition to "the modern epoch." See her *John Milton*, 8-12. My definition of the transitional nature of Milton's early poetry, however, is at once more specific in its terms and more general in its application.

14. Norbrook, *Poetry and Politics*, 283; Wilding, "Milton's Early Radicalism," in *John Milton*, ed. Patterson, 39 and 45, and *Dragons Teeth*, 73-75. Curiously, neither Wilding nor Norbrook mentions Howard Dobin's political reading of the *Nativity Ode* as an antiroyalist masque in "Milton's *Nativity Ode:* 'O What a Mask Was There,'" *Milton Quarterly* 17 (1983): 71-80.

1. THE POETRY OF ABSENCE

1. Barker, "Pattern of Milton's *Nativity Ode*," 170.

2. Woodhouse, "Milton's Early Development," 73.

3. Tuve, *Five Poems by Milton*, 44; Barker, "Pattern of Milton's *Nativity Ode*," 170.

4. Cullen, "Imitation and Metamorphosis," 1568.

5. MacLaren, "Milton's *Nativity Ode*," 1629," 194.

6. Christopher, *Science of the Saints*, 23.

7. Shafer, *English Ode to 1660*; Shuster, *English Ode from Milton to Keats*; Maddison, *Apollo and the Nine*; Fry, *Poet's Calling*; Rollinson, "Milton's Nativity Poem."

8. Shafer, *English Ode to 1660*, 17; Fry, *Poet's Calling*, 44.

9. In order to maintain her thesis that the poem is spoken by a "poet-swain," Georgia Christopher is forced to rewrite line 27 to read "and join [his] voice unto the Angel Choir" (*Science of the Saints*, 23). Similarly, Michael Lieb asserts that "the speaker desires to 'lay' his 'humble ode' lowly at [Christ's] blessed feet" ("Milton and the Kenotic Christology," 352). In his article "Miltonic Narration: Christ's Nativity," Frank S. Kastor also states repeatedly that Milton "places himself at the scene."

10. Cf. William Kerrigan's reference to "the composite voice of the *Nativity Ode*" in *The Prophetic Milton*, 200.

11. Ransom, "A Poem Nearly Anonymous." Richard Halpern's more recent theory that Milton "appropriates the occasion of Christ's birth to announce his own poetic nativity" also assumes that the poem is essentially autobiographical ("The Great Instauration," 6).

12. Barker, "Pattern of Milton's *Nativity Ode*," 181.

13. Halpern, "The Great Instauration," 6-7.

14. See the first two illustrations in Keynes, ed., *On the Morning of Christ's Nativity*.

15. Nelson, *Baroque Lyric Poetry*, 41-52.

16. Belsey, *John Milton*, 5.

17. Virgil, *Eclogue IV*, lines 8-9. I quote from the text and translation of the eclogues printed in H.R. Fairclough, *Virgil with an English Translation* (Cambridge: Harvard Univ. Press, 1967). All subsequent references to the *Eclogues* are to this edition, cited by line number only.

18. Rand, "Milton in Rustication," 129.

19. Cullen, "Imitation and Metamorphosis," 1565. As John Rumrich has remarked in personal correspondence with me, it might be more accurate to describe the *Nativity Ode* as a fulfillment rather than a prophecy, for it describes the event that was supposedly prophesied in *Eclogue IV*, the birth of the redeemer. In this respect Milton's poem bears something of the same relationship to its Roman predecessor as the New Testament does to the Old in the Christian theory of typology.

20. For a detailed study of the subject see Mayor, *Virgil's Messianic Eclogue*.

21. Augustine, *Epistle to the Romans*, 1.3, quoted in Rose, *Eclogues of Vergil*, chapter 8.

22. Dante, "Purgatorio," 22.67-73. I quote throughout from the translation of the *Divine Comedy* in Dorothy L. Sayers, trans., *The Comedy of Dante Alighieri* (London: Penguin, 1949-62). For an iconographical example of the messianic tradition see Giovanni di Stefano's remarkable rendering of the Cumaean Sibyl on the floor of Siena Cathedral.

23. Lisle, introduction to *Eclogue IV*, in *Virgil's Eclogues*, 60.

24. Lisle, introduction to *Eclogue IV*, in *Virgil's Eclogues*, 68-70.

25. Fletcher, *Christs Triumph Over Death*, vol. 1, lines 49-56.

26. See Allen, *Mysteriously Meant*, and Bush, *Mythology and the Renaissance Tradition*.

27. Donne, *A Sermon*, 9.

28. Eburne, *Plaine Pathway*, 59.

29. Purchas, *Purchas His Pilgrimes*, 1816-18.

30. White, *Planter's Plea*, 19.

31. Kendrick, "Milton and Sexuality," 45. Michael Wilding also suggests that the pagan gods in the last third of the poem are connected with the corrupt clergy whose "ruin" Milton claimed to have predicted in *Lycidas*. See Wilding, *Dragons Teeth*, 15-16.

32. See Patrides, "Cessation of the Oracles."

33. Prudentius, *Apotheosis*, 1:153-55, lines 402-46.

34. Grierson, *First Half*, 182; Carey, *Poems of John Milton*, 98.

35. Nock, *Conversion*, 7.

36. See James, *Varieties of Religious Experience*.

37. Ephesians 4:22-24. See also Colossians 3:9-10. All biblical citations are from the Authorized Version.

38. Milton, *CW*, 15:366. Milton's authorship of *De Doctrina* has been vigorously challenged by William B. Hunter in "The Provenance of the *Christian Doctrine*," *Studies in English Literature* 32 (1992): 129-42, and is currently under investigation by a distinguished committee. The correspondences between the prose tract and the poems I discuss are so close, however, that in the absence of convincing evidence to the contrary I will assume in what follows that the traditional attribution is correct.

39. Tertullian, *De Praescr.*, 7; Jerome, *Epist.*, 22.29.

40. See, for instance, Regina M. Schwartz, *Remembering and Repeating*, chapter 1.

41. Milton, *CW*, 3:223-24.

42. Augustine, *On Christian Doctrine*, 2:40.

43. Romans 6:6.

44. John Calvin, *Praelection on Jeremiah*, 31.18, quoted in Richardson, *Dictionary of Christian Theology*, 74.

45. Smith, "Milton's Method of Mistakes."

46. Cullen, "Imitation and Metamorphosis," 1567.

47. Empson, *Some Versions of Pastoral*, 174. Cf. Kerrigan's observation that "Milton presents the sunrise . . . as if it were a sunset" (*The Prophetic Milton*, 227).

48. Laurence H. Jacobs observes in "'Unexpressive Notes': The Decorum of Milton's *Nativity Ode*" that the phrase "anticipates the burial of Jesus" (175).

49. Rajan, "In Order Serviceable," 13.

50. Meier, "Sectarian Discord, 7."

51. James, *Varieties of Religious Experience*, 209.

52. Milton, *CW*, 15:115.

2. Virtue and Virginity

1. Adams, *Milton and the Modern Critics*, 12-13.

2. I assume both here and in what follows that the text of *Comus* preserved in the Bridgewater MS is the closest we are ever likely to get to the version of the masque performed at Ludlow in 1634.

3. Adams, *Milton and the Modern Critics*, 3.

4. Brown, *John Milton's Aristocratic Entertainments*; Creaser, "Milton's *Comus*"; Shawcross, "MSS. of *Comus*" and "Dating of the Trinity MS."; Smith, "Milton's Revisions"; Sprott, *John Milton, A Maske*.

5. See Sprott, *John Milton, A Maske*, introduction.

6. Aristotle, *Nichomachean Ethics*, 2.2.35-36. I quote throughout from the translation by Ostwald (Indianapolis: Bobbs-Merrill, 1962), in which the Greek *sophrosyne* is consistently rendered as "self-control." In all the Latin translations of Aristotle's treatise that I have consulted, as well as in the English translations available in the Renaissance, *sophrosyne* appears as *temperantia* or "temperance." In the body of this chapter, "temperance," "moderation," and "self-control" are used interchangeably.

7. Kerrigan, *The Sacred Complex*, 27-28.

8. Kerrigan, *The Sacred Complex*, 28.

9. Barker, *Puritan Dilemma*, 10-11.

10. Plato, *Phaedo*, trans. F.J. Church (Indianapolis: Bobbs-Merrill, 1951), 66. All subsequent quotations are from this version.

11. Brown, *John Milton's Aristocratic Entertainments*, 141, 58; my emphasis. Kendrick performs a similar act of verbal legerdemain when he describes the Lady's encounter with Comus: "To Comus's voluptuous, neo-aristocratic argument for temperance [*sic*], the Lady first responds by citing the social effects of a stern moderation; such chastity would produce a disciplined society" ("Milton and Sexuality," 65).

12. The quoted phrase is Kendrick's ("Milton and Sexuality," 53, 63). Neither Kendrick nor Kerrigan, however, addresses the incompatibility between virginity and temperance, Kerrigan because he does not "understand why conflicts of affect or proposition in a work should be prima facie evidence of 'disunity,' or if so, why disunity should be considered prima facie a flaw" (*The Sacred Complex*, 29), Kendrick because he apparently believes that Comus is the proponent of temperance (see n. 11).

13. Leah S. Marcus, "Milieu of Milton's *Comus*," 318. Cf. Woodhouse's comment in "The Argument of Milton's *Comus*": "That the doctrine of chastity is the central theme in the argument of the poem is obvious from the emphasis that it receives" (52).

14. Shawcross, *Self and the World*, 51-52. See also Angus Fletcher's discussion of chastity and virginity in *The Transcendental Masque: An Essay on Milton's "Comus,"* 209-21.

15. Shawcross, *Self and the World*, 51. See also John G. Demaray, *Milton and the Masque Tradition*, 93.

16. The Lady would "something say" (283) to Comus because he has disparaged "chastity," but since he is incapable of understanding the concept of "virginity" there would be no point in doing so. If chastity means something other than virginity here, her argument makes no sense. See Adams, *Milton and the Modern Critics*, 9: "the Lady uses the 'Sun-clad power of Chastity' as a synonym for the 'doctrine of Virginity.'"

17. Christopher, *Science of the Saints*, 43, 36-37.
18. McGuire, *Milton's Puritan Masque*, 172, 138, 169.
19. Kerrigan, *The Sacred Complex*, 33.
20. Plato, *Phaedo*, 31.
21. Breasted, "*Comus* and the Castlehaven Scandal"; Marcus, "Milieu of Milton's *Comus.*"
22. Tillyard, "The Action of *Comus*," in *Studies in Milton*, 97. In this summary of the temptation scene Tillyard ignores the fact that long before the Attendant Spirit "gives the solution" in his epilogue the Lady has advocated "the Aristotelian middle course" in her reply to Comus.
23. Macklem, "Love, Nature, and Grace."
24. Tillyard, "The Action of *Comus*," 47; Macklem, "Love, Nature, and Grace," 540.
25. Tillyard, "The Action of *Comus*," 44.
26. Macklem, "Love, Nature, and Grace," 539-40.
27. Rajan, *The Lofty Rhyme*, 35.
28. The primacy of temperance is even clearer in Milton's original version of the temptation scene in Trinity 1, where, as I noted earlier, the invitation to drink Comus's cordial julep came at the end rather than the beginning of his encounter with the Lady. The tempter's theoretical arguments were only the prelude to the concrete temptation of the enchanted cup, which thus became the moral focus of the entire scene. In Milton's revisions, however, the offer of the cup became a mere preliminary to the attack on abstinence.
29. See, for example, Arthur O. Lovejoy, *The Great Chain of Being*, and Tillyard, *The Elizabethan World Picture*.
30. Dante, *Divine Comedy*, "Paradiso," 3.73-75.
31. Castiglione, *The Book of the Courtier*, trans. Charles S. Singleton (New York: Anchor, 1959), 302. All subsequent quotations from Castiglione's treatise are from this version.
32. More, *Thomas More: Utopia*, trans. H.V.S. Ogden, 74.
33. Lovejoy discusses the same basic tension but attributes it to two different conceptions of the Creator: "There was no way in which the flight from the Many to the One, the quest of a perfection defined wholly in terms of contrast with the created world, could be effectually harmonized with the imitation of a Goodness that delights in diversity and manifests itself in the emanation of the Many out of the One. The one program demanded a withdrawal from all "attachment to creatures" and culminated in the ecstatic contemplation of the indivisible Divine Essence; the other, if it had been formulated, would have summoned men to participate in some finite measure in the creative passion of God, to collaborate consciously in the processes by

which the diversity of things, the fullness of the universe is achieved" (*Great Chain of Being*, 83-84; see also 96).

34. Milton, *On the Death of a Fair Infant Dying of a Cough*, line 63.

35. Milton, *Nativity Ode*, line 14.

36. Milton, *On Time*, lines 19-20. See also *Prolusion 2*, where Milton notes, "we shall never be permitted to enjoy [the music of the spheres] so long as we remain brutish and overwhelmed by wicked animal desires," and *Prolusion 3*, where he adds, "Certainly divine Poetry, . . . rousing to high flight the mind, buried in earthly dross, establishes quarters among the temples of the sky" (*CW*, 12:157, 163).

37. A.S.P. Woodhouse posits an intermediate zone between the realm of grace and the realm of nature, but there is no textual evidence that Milton believed in such an arrangement. See Woodhouse, "Milton's *Comus*."

38. Cedric Brown argues that the Elder Brother's speech is naively optimistic: "The Platonic doctrine of ascent glosses over what were for Milton the facts of man's position in a world still dominated by the fight against active evil" (*John Milton's Aristocratic Entertainments*, 101). It seems to me implausible, however, that Milton would have put into the mouth of the Earl of Bridgewater's son and heir sentiments that he himself believed were unrealistic.

39. Reesing, *Milton's Poetic Art*, 5; Rajan, *The Lofty Rhyme*, 27.

40. For the Platonic and neo-Platonic elements in *Comus* see Sears Jayne, "Milton's Ludlow Mask," and John Arthos, "Milton, Ficino, and the Charmides."

41. Milton, *CW*, 3:66. Comus's cup, of course, was not "a thing indifferent," and that is why the Lady cannot drink from it even in moderation.

42. Milton, *CW*, 3:281.

43. Milton, *CW*, 3:431. Cf. *Colasterion*, where Milton repeats the initial simile word-for-word and then points out that "gravest authors, both Aristotle in the second of his *Ethics* to *Nichomachus*, and *Seneca* in his seventh *De Beneficiis*, advise us to stretch out the line of precept oft times beyond measure, that while wee tend furder, the mean might bee the easier attain'd" (*CW*, 4:259).

44. Milton, *CW*, 4:311, my emphasis. Over the course of the centuries the word "temperance" itself has undergone just such a semantic shift in common parlance. The members of a modern "temperance society," for instance, are dedicated not to the moderate consumption of alcohol but to total abstinence.

45. Diekhoff, "A Maske at Ludlow," in *Maske at Ludlow*, ed. Diekhoff, 14.

46. Adams, *Milton and the Modern Critics,* 27.

47. Brooks and Hardy, eds., *Poems of Mr. John Milton,* 233.

48. Whiting, *Milton and This Pendant World,* 19.

49. Dyson, "The Interpretation of *Comus,*" in *Maske at Ludlow,* ed. Diekhoff, 103.

50. Kristeller, *Renaissance Thought,* chapter 1.

51. Castiglione, *Book of the Courtier,* 295.

52. Milton, *CW,* 4:277

53. Milton, *CW,* 4:311.

54. Madsen, "Nature in Milton's Poetry," 216.

55. Adams, *Milton and the Modern Critics,* 17-18.

56. Norbrook, *Poetry and Politics,* 261.

57. Virtually all those critics who follow Brooks and Hardy in interpreting the final lines as a positive reference to the descent of grace invoke the example of the Attendant Spirit. To quote only the most recent instance, Michael Wilding concludes his chapter on "Comus, Camus, Commerce" by observing that "the descent of the Attendant Spirit to help the Lady has been the enactment of Heaven's stooping" (*Dragons Teeth,* 88). See also Brown, *John Milton's Aristocratic Entertainments,* 3.

58. The result is a rather curious ambiguity concerning Thyrsis's true nature. As he tells us, he is only impersonating "a Swain / That to this house belongs" (84-85), yet he is being played by a "shepherd" who really did belong to the Bridgewater household. The real Thyrsis, as it were, was impersonating a spirit who was impersonating the real Thyrsis.

59. As John Shawcross has pointed out in private correspondence, Milton subsequently played the role of a teacher himself. After his return from Italy he tutored his nephews, Edward and Christopher Phillips, and he devoted numerous prose works to essentially educational projects: *Of Education, The History of Britain, The Art of Logic, Accedence Commenc't Grammar,* and *A Brief History of Moscovia.*

60. See Jeanne S. Martin, "Transformations of Genre."

61. Lactantius's third step, abstaining from evil thoughts, Milton would have regarded as impossible. Even before the Fall, "Evil into the mind of God or Man / May come or go, so unapprov'd, and leave / No spot or blame behind" (*Paradise Lost,* 5.117-19).

3. THE ROAD FROM HORTON

1. Levinson, *Seasons,* 85. In *John Milton: The Self and the World,* John Shawcross argues persuasively that "Autumn 1637 was the turning point in Milton's career" (95), the period in which he finally aban-

doned his clerical ambitions and committed himself to a career as a poet (67, 64). Although I am not sure that either decision (especially the second) can be dated quite so precisely, I assume in what follows that both decisions were made before the composition of *Lycidas* in November of the same year.

2. Woodhouse and Bush, *Variorum Commentary*, 2.2.652.

3. Miles, "Primary Language of *Lycidas*."

4. Sacks, *English Elegy*, 25. Cf. Angus Fletcher's discussion of "the principle of echo" and "typological repetition" in *The Transcendental Masque*, 198-209, 219-26.

5. See Michael Lieb, "'Yet Once More'"; Edward W. Tayler, "*Lycidas* in Christian Time," in *Lycidas: The Tradition and the Poem*, ed. Patrides, 303-18; and J.A. Wittreich, *Visionary Poetics*, 138-41 and 150-52.

6. Romans 5:19.

7. Adams, "Death and Rebirth in *Lycidas*."

8. Bloom, *The Anxiety of Influence*, 30.

9. Martz, "Who is Lycidas?" 170. After reviewing Lycidas's appearance in Theocritus's seventh *Idyl*, Virgil's ninth *Eclogue*, and Sannazaro's *Phyllis*, Martz concludes that "the name Lycidas . . . prepares us from the outset for the poem's movement beyond the limitations of the pastoral elegy into the broader reaches of the pastoral eclogue with its awareness of the world of history" (187). My analysis will be more concerned with the ironic relationship between Milton's protagonist and his namesakes.

10. Woodhouse and Bush, *Variorum Commentary*, 637. In her note "Milton's Lycidas: New Light on the Title," Joanne M. Riley suggests that Lycidas's name is connected with the Greek *lusis* (deliverance, liberation). In fact the name derives from the Greek *lukis* (wolf) and means "the wolf's son." In view of his use of the wolf in line 128 it seems unlikely, however, that Milton would have wished to remind his readers of this derivation.

11. Kirkconnell, *Awake the Courteous Echo*, 91 n. 26.

12. In his edition, *John Milton: Complete Poems and Major Prose*, Merritt Y. Hughes incorrectly states that Menalcas is one of the competitors in *Idyl VII* (136).

13. Putnam, *Virgil's Pastoral Art*.

14. Theocritus, *Idyl VII*, trans. Harrison, lines 52-62.

15. The irony is reinforced by the two Renaissance elegies most closely resembling Milton's: Jacob Sannazaro's *Phyllis* (1526), in which Lycidas is a fisherman bewailing the death of a young woman he loved, and Giles Fletcher the Elder's *Adonis* (1576), in which he is a spokesman for the poet mourning the death of Clere Haddon, who was

drowned in the Cam. Once again the roles are reversed in *Lycidas*. The figure who stood weeping on the seashore or the riverbank is now buried under the "whelming tide" (157), himself the occasion for an elegy.

16. Putnam, *Virgil's Pastoral Art*, 300.

17. Putnam, *Virgil's Pastoral Art*, 338.

18. As I have pointed out in "Lycidas, Daphnis, and Gallus," Virgil's adaptation of *Idyl I* shaped the Renaissance interpretation of the Greek poem to such an extent that the two poems virtually coalesced. On the relationship between *Lycidas* and *Idyl I* see my monograph, *The Road from Horton*, and J.H. Hanford, "The Pastoral Elegy and Milton's *Lycidas*."

19. Melanchthon, *Argumenta*, signature G8.

20. Brinsley, *Virgil's Eclogues*, 98, 95. Cf. Ramus, *P. Virgilii Maronis Bucolica*, 166. Brinsley evidently knew Ramus's commentary well and did not hesitate to borrow interpretations from it.

21. Melanchthon, *Argumenta*, signature G6r. Only the first of Melanchthon's analyses treats the poem in allegorical terms. The remaining five are rigorously literal.

22. Lisle, *Virgil's Eclogues*, 184; Lisle is translating Vives, *Io Ludovico Vivis*, 34.

23. Revelation 14.

24. Sacks, *English Elegy*, 93

25. Mayerson, "Orpheus Image in *Lycidas*."

26. Cain, "Renaissance Orpheus"; Davidson, "Milton, Orpheus, and Poetry"; DuRocher, *Milton and Ovid*, 64-74; Friedman, *Orpheus;* Hollander, *Untuning of the Sky;* Walker, "Orpheus the Theologian"; Williamson, "Myth of Orpheus"; Adams, "Death and Rebirth in *Lycidas*"; Fraser, "Approaches to *Lycidas*"; Frye, "Milton's *Lycidas*"; Tuve, "Theme, Pattern, and Imagery."

27. Tuve, "Theme, Pattern, and Imagery," 189.

28. Mayerson, "Orpheus Image in *Lycidas*," 124; Adams, "Death and Rebirth in *Lycidas*," 115.

29. Fraser, "Approaches to *Lycidas*," 40. Fraser's christological interpretation is vulnerable, however, to the obvious objection that it does not differentiate between similarities and dissimilarities. Once the initial relationship between the two figures has been established, parallels and contrasts alike become grist to Fraser's analogizing mill. Thus, the fact that Orpheus resembled Christ in descending into hell is adduced as evidence in support of the same conclusion as is the fact that Orpheus differed from Christ in returning from hell empty-handed. With a critical method like that, virtually any character in the entire corpus of classical mythology could be transformed into a "kind

of prefiguration of Christ." My own critical method here, I realize, also draws attention both to the resemblances and to the differences between Edward King and the various figures Milton compares him with. My objection to Fraser's analysis is that he does not discriminate between the two kinds of relationship.

30. This shift in emphasis was facilitated by the fact that Ovid had split the story into two separate sections in his *Metamorphoses*. Orpheus's descent into the underworld is related in Book 10, his subsequent adventures in Book 11. Medieval commentators who emphasized the christological implications of the former, it should be noted, at least did so more consistently than some of their modern successors. Confronted by the differences between Christ and Orpheus noted by Fraser, Pierre Bersuire, for example, attempted to bring the pagan legend into conformity with Christian teaching by giving it a happy ending; in his *Metamorfosis Ovidiana moraliter explanata* Orpheus succeeds in bringing Eurydice back from the underworld. In the seventeenth century, on the other hand, Alexander Ross made the contrast between the two quests the occasion for affirming Christ's superiority. "What was in vain attempted by Orpheus," he declared in his *Mystagogus Poeticus*, "was performed by our Saviour, for he alone hath delivered our soules from the nethermost hell" (339).

31. Cain, "Renaissance Orpheus," 25.

32. DuRocher, *Milton and Ovid*, 70

33. Giles Fletcher's treatment of the story in *Christs Victorie and Triumph* is unusual in preserving the medieval christological version of the myth.

34. Mayerson, "Orpheus Image in *Lycidas*," 194. Of the four episodes in Orpheus's life which, according to Cain, were most often treated by the humanists, none includes the Bacchantes' assault. Interestingly enough, it is this final section of the legend that Milton's nephew, Edward Phillips, emphasizes in his account of Orpheus's life in *The New World of English Words*.

35. Cain, "Renaissance Orpheus," 25.

36. Critics disagree about the date of *Ad Patrem*. The editors of the *Variorum* think that it was written as early as 1631; Grierson and Tillyard believe that it was composed not long before 1637; and John Shawcross dates it in early March, 1638. In view of the parallels in phraseology with *Lycidas*, the later dates seem to me more probable, though, unlike Shawcross, I believe it was written before the elegy. The parallel between the "inenarrabile carmen" that Milton mentions to his father and the "unexpressive nuptial Song" (176) overheard by Edward King has often been noticed, but there are many other similarities between the two works in both phraseology and conception.

The opening description of the Muse "meditating" (7) her song in *Ad Patrem* anticipates the poet's obligation to "meditate" (66) the Muse in *Lycidas;* "aurea Clio" (14) has her counterpart in the "golden hayrd Calliope" of Milton's original draft for the later poem; the account of Olympus adumbrates most of the features that characterize "the blest Kingdoms meek of joy and love" (177); the ivy and laurel of the victor's crown reappear as the symbols of Bacchus and Apollo; and the youthful poet who is no longer content to remain "obscurus" (103) survives as the "uncouth Swain" (186) mourning for Lycidas.

37. Williamson finds an analogous difference in the use of the myth in *L'Allegro* and in *Il Penseroso.*

38. Ovid, *Metamorphoses*, 10.79-11.43. Cf. Virgil, *Georgics*, 4.507-527.

39. Mayerson, "Orpheus Image in *Lycidas*," 190; Woodhouse and Bush, *Variorum Commentary*, 657. Cf. Eric Smith's observation in *By Mourning Tongues: Studies in English Elegy* that Orpheus was killed "by the Bacchantes in jealousy of his faithfulness to his dead wife Eurydice" (27).

40. Boethius, *Consolation of Philosophy*, bk. 3 sect. 12. Cf. Salutati's interpretation of the story, quoted in Friedman, *Orpheus*, 144, and Trivet's comments, quoted in Hollander, *Untuning of the Sky*, 88 n. 60.

41. Quoted in Friedman, *Orpheus*, 123.

42. Quoted in Friedman, *Orpheus*, 120.

43. Quoted in Cain, "Renaissance Orpheus," 26-27.

44. Bacon, *Wisdom of the Ancients*, in J. Spedding et al., eds., *Sir Francis Bacon: The Works*, 6:172.

45. George Sandys, *Ovid's Metamorphoses Englished, Mythologiz'd and Represented in Figures*, 387.

46. See under "Orpheus" in *Dictionarium Historicum et Poeticum.* The idea that Orpheus preached against marriage seems to have been a medieval addition to the story. See Friedman, *Orpheus*, 171.

47. Interestingly enough, Orpheus was directly associated with Gallus in at least two Renaissance commentaries. According to Servius, Virgil had originally concluded his fourth *Georgic* with a eulogy to his fellow poet, but was ordered by Caesar Augustus to omit it when Gallus fell from favor in 26 B.C. In its place Virgil inserted the fable of Aristaeus, which culminates in the Orpheus episode. By the sixteenth century Servius's anecdote was taken to mean that Virgil had simply substituted a covert for an overt tribute to Gallus, praising him, in Melanchthon's words, "sub fabula Aristei" (*Argumenta*, signature G7). Cf. Abraham Fleming, *Bucolicks of Publius Virgilius Maro*, 29.

48. Brinsley, *Virgil's Eclogues*, 95.

49. Sacks, *English Elegy*, 105.

50. Tuve, "Theme, Pattern, and Imagery," 189.

51. DuRocher, *Milton and Ovid*, 71.

52. See Sacks, *English Elegy:* "He would now have to question and renegotiate the supposed exchange by which renunciation buys its own reward and self-sacrifice defends against mortality" (94).

53. Jonson, *Volpone*, 3.7.165-66.

54. In his article "The Development of the Flower Passage in Lycidas," H.H. Adams argues that Milton revised these lines because he realized that the "sensual" overtones he had given the image of the primrose were "completely inappropriate." It seems to me, nevertheless, that the original version of the passage provides interesting evidence concerning Milton's state of mind while he was writing the poem. At this point of his life he seems to have been especially sensitive to the pathos of "uninjoyed love." Cf. his reference in the *Elegia Prima* to the "unhappy boy" who "leaves joys untasted, and falls in death through the rending of his love" (41-42), and his description in the *Epitaphium Damonis* of the "unwedded" grapes which wither with "their clusters neglected" (65).

55. LeComte, *Yet Once More*, 6.

56. Cf. Milton's strategy of simultaneous allusion to multiple sources in the title and in the address to the nymphs, not to mention in the multiple allusions to Revelation in lines 165-81.

57. J.M. French argues in his article on "The Digressions in Milton's *Lycidas*" that there is also a structural parallel between Milton's questions here and St. Peter's attack on the clergy. "Amaryllis," he writes, "has been metamorphosed into ecclesiastical sinecure but the principle is the same."

58. In *Paradise Lost*, as several commentators have noted, the process of poetic inspiration is described in terms that suggest the act of insemination. LeComte has also noted a "sly equation" between poetic inspiration and male potency in *Elegia V* ("Sly Milton," 7). It may also be worth noting in this context that Henry Lawes referred to *Comus* as Milton's "off-spring" in the anonymous edition of 1637.

59. The tumescent implications of raising the "clear spirit" are obvious, especially when we remember that in the seventeenth century the word "spirit" could mean, among other things, semen (cf. the opening pun in Shakespeare's sonnet "The expense of spirit in a waste of shame"). The "fair guerdon" to which it aspires could well be a courtly euphemism for the usual reward bestowed by merciful ladies upon their faithful lovers. And it would be hard to improve upon the phrase "burst out into sudden blaze" as a description of an orgasm. On the theme of castration in *Lycidas* see Sacks, *English Elegy*, 96, 102, and 109.

60. Why, however, the blind fury and not the blind fate? Milton was too good a classicist to be unaware that it was Atropos, not Megaera or one of her sisters, who held the fatal shears. No one, to the best of my knowledge, has yet offered a satisfactory explanation for this extraordinary conflation.

61. Lines 3-4. The association of "ears" with "shears" may be more than a matter of rhyme. William Prynne had recently had the former chopped off by the latter, as Milton still remembered almost ten years later, in his sonnet "On the New Forcers of Conscience."

62. Donald M. Friedman comments on this episode: "The question he asks himself is not simply whether one kind of poetry is better than another, but whether the kind of poetry he knows to be better is worth pursuing if his labors and his achieved excellence are never to be given due praise" (*Orpheus*, 12). This, surely, is to read the answer back into the question. The swain says nothing about "achieved excellence" in lines 64-76. His concern is, rather, the possibility that he will never be given the opportunity to achieve the excellence his self-discipline deserves.

63. Cooper, see under "Orpheus" in *Dictionarium Historicum et Poeticum*.

64. The reference to the death of Hyacinth reminds us that Phoebus was a lover too. In addition to the obvious visual similarities between Camus and Silvanus there may also be a thematic connection. According to Ramus and Brinsley, Silvanus's ferulas came from "a kind of shrub or big herbe like unto fennel giant, with the branches whereof schoole-masters used to iert children on the hands, whence came the name of Ferula" (Brinsley, *Virgil's Eclogues*, 95; Ramus, *P. Virgilii Maronis Bucolica*, 163). If there is any truth to Aubrey's story that Milton was beaten by his tutor, William Chappell, it is easy to see how such an etymology might have created a chain of association leading from Silvanus to the representative of Cambridge University.

65. In addition to its usual meaning, "pledge" can also mean "child"; see Woodhouse and Bush, *Variorum Commentary*, 672. Milton also uses the phrase "reverend Sire" to describe Samson's father, Manoa, in *Samson Agonistes* (326). As we have just seen, Phoebus was generally believed to have been the father of King's mythic surrogate, Orpheus.

66. Cf. *Nativity Ode*, 88-90.

67. Pan's "blood-red elderberries" may have suggested Camus's "sanguine flower."

68. Riccius, *Paraphrases, Ecphrases, succintae quaestiones*, signature M7v.

69. If, however, the "two-handed engine" refers to what Milton was to call the "wholesome and preventive shears" of parliament, with

its two houses, as some scholars have suggested, then the addition to the headnote would be entirely accurate. For Michael's sword, see Revelation 1:16 and 19:15. In *Paradise Lost* Michael's sword smites his adversaries "with huge two-handed sway" (6.251).

70. That Milton himself was troubled by such questions appears all the more likely when we follow the advice of several commentators and compare St. Peter's condemnation of "our corrupted Clergie" with his fiery imprecations against the papacy in the *Divine Comedy* ("Paradiso," 27.54-63). A millennial solution to a contemporary problem would never satisfy Dante's St. Peter. Providence, he maintains, cannot remain aloof for very much longer; unless it acts "soon," the wolves will devour the entire flock.

71. Shawcross, *Self and the World*, 68. Cf. James Holly Hanford's observation that "the rebuke administered to the corrupt clergy is an echo of [Milton's] own determination not to go into the church" (*A Milton Handbook*, 4th ed. (New York: Appleton-Century-Crofts, 1946), 168).

72. Milton, *CW*, 3:242.

73. I have given my reasons for rejecting Hill's assumption in my review of his book in *Review of English Studies*, n.s., 31 (l98l): 354-55.

74. Milton, *CW*, 12:320-25.

75. Milton, *Elegia VI*, 55-66. In a number of respects, Milton's early conception of the poet had more in common with the Catholic than with the Protestant notion of a priest. He was expected, for instance, to be chaste, and he served as a divinely appointed intermediary between God and man.

76. Auden, "In Memory of W.B. Yeats," 36-37.

77. See French, "Digressions in Milton's *Lycidas*," 485-90. From a psychological point of view, too, St. Peter's speech is thoroughly pertinent. In the face of the premature death of a young and promising human being, we naturally ask: why did it have to be him or her rather than someone else? In Lear's words, "Why should a dog, a horse, a rat have life, / And thou no breath at all?" (5.3.306-7).

78. Alpers, "Eclogue Tradition," 353.

79. Friedman, "Swain's Paideia." Friedman reads *Lycidas* in much the same way that Arthur Barker interpreted the *Nativity Ode*, as a record of the poet's conversion and self-dedication.

80. Milton quotes this phrase word-for-word in the *Epitaphium Damonis*, line 71.

81. For this reason, if for no other, it seems extremely unlikely that the dolphins which are summoned to waft Milton's "hapless youth" (164) could be related to the music-loving mammal which carried Arion to safety. As I have argued in "Lycidas and the Dolphins," Milton was

probably referring neither to Arion's savior nor to the bearer of Melicertes's dead body in Pausanias's *Descriptio Graecae*, but to the troop of dolphins which carried the corpse of the Greek poet Hesiod back to shore in Plutarch's *Septem sapientium convivium*.

82. See Don Cameron Allen, *The Harmonious Vision*, 47-52.

83. The legalistic language of Phoebus's description—"witness," "all-judging" (82)—implies the metaphor of a judicial proceeding.

84. Revelation 14:2-4, 19:6-7. In his paper "Milton's Vow of Celibacy," John Leonard takes exception to my ellipsis, pointing out quite rightly that "it overleaps five whole chapters of Revelation" (192). It is my contention, however, that the two passages coalesced in Milton's imagination here, as they did again in the *Epitaphium Damonis*. Indeed, as Leonard himself notes, Milton immediately goes on to add a phrase from Revelation 7:17 and 21:4—"God shall wipe away all tears from their eyes"—to his fusion of Revelation 14 and 19.

85. *Elegia Tertia*, 59-64; *At a Solemn Music*, 6-16; *Ad Patrem*, 30-37; *Epitaphium Damonis*, 212-17; *Reason of Church Government*, *CW*, 3:238; *Apology for Smectymnuus*, *CW*, 3:306.

86. Milton, *CW*, 3:238.

87. Milton, *CW*, 3:306.

88. The *Apology* was published only a month or two before Milton's marriage. One of the most influential Protestant commentators of the Renaissance, David Pareus, contended in his *Commentary Upon the Divine Revelation of the Apostle and Evangelist John* that "this place serves neither to disgrace the marriage estate nor to establish the merit of corporal virginity" (334). For detailed studies of Puritan attitudes toward the interpretation of the Apocalypse, see Michael Fixler, *Milton and the Kingdoms of God*, and Austin C. Dobbins, *Milton and the Book of Revelation: The Heavenly Cycle*.

89. Pareus, *Divine Revelation*, 334.

90. Leonard asserts that St. John's vision of the undefiled virgins here does not necessarily imply that the passage "voices a personal program of [sexual] inaction," because Milton is mourning the death of an unmarried man, and the vision consequently "provides a particularly apt consolation in the circumstances" ("Milton's Vow of Celibacy," 198). But Edward King too had died unmarried, so a reference to the virgins would have been equally apt in his case. What is more, whether or not *torus* in Milton's original Latin means a marriage bed, or simply a bed, as Leonard argues, the passage in the *Epitaphium Damonis* introduces the undefiled virgins into the marriage of the Lamb in exactly the same way as I believe the passage in *Lycidas* did.

91. Ficino, Preface to Dionysius the Areopagite's *Mystical Theology*, quoted in Edgar Wind, *Pagan Mysteries*, 62; my emphasis.

92. In the original Latin, Ficino and Milton use almost the same verb to describe the actions of the revelers: *debacchantur* (Ficino), *bacchantur* (Milton).

93. Alpers, "Eclogue Tradition," 371. In a similar vein, Fish comments that the final lines are "perfectly, that is unrelievedly, conventional" ("A Poem Finally Anonymous," 339).

94. Hanford, "Pastoral Elegy," 43; Hughes, ed., *John Milton: Complete Poems and Major Prose*, 125. See also Eric Smith, *By Mourning Tongues*, 138, and Ralph W. Condee's comment in *Structure in Milton's Poetry:* "The whole passage parallels the conclusion of Virgil's tenth eclogue, which sings the sorrow of Gallus" (39). Less often noted is the fact that both the first *Idyl* and the tenth *Eclogue* conclude with a direct reference to the animals that the singer has in his care. Significantly, perhaps, there is no mention of the flock at the end of *Lycidas*.

95. Brooks and Hardy, eds., *Poems of Mr. John Milton*, 151. The asymmetry of the ending is not always recognized, however. For instance, in his essay on "Milton's Pastoral Monodies," A.S.P. Woodhouse writes: "*Lycidas* commences with a prelude which is part of the monody but which is to be balanced by the brief Epilogue, so that together they give something of the effect of the traditional framework setting" (273). A.E. Barker's famous analysis of the tripartite nature of the poem also implies that the epilogue is balanced by a prologue, as does the widespread use of the word "framing" to describe the conclusion of *Lycidas*.

96. Ransom, "A Poem Nearly Anonymous."

97. Battestin, "Ransom and *Lycidas*", 227

98. In "*Lycidas*" *and the Italian Critics* Clay Hunt argues that Milton employs the term in the sense it had come to have in the new music of the period, that is, "a musical declamation *in stilo recitativo* for a solo voice" (163). In either case, the dramatic character of the monody is still its dominant feature.

99. The distinctiveness of Milton's final stanza emerges even more clearly if we compare it with its other major analogue, the conclusion of canto 6 of Phineas Fletcher's *Purple Island:* "But see, the stealing night with softly pace / To flie the western sunne, creeps up the east; / Cold Hesper 'gins unmask his evening face; / And calls the winking starres from drouzie rest: / Home then my lambes; the falling drops eschew: / To morrow shal ye feast in pastures new, / And with the rising sunne banquet on pearled dew." After pointing out the obvious parallels in theme and phraseology, G.S. Fraser remarks that "the most surprising resemblance is a much broader one; the tone, mood, and pace of Fletcher's passage are very like Milton, and indeed one would have said typically Miltonic" ("Approaches to *Lycidas*, 37). The overall

effect, however, is the exact converse. Fletcher's stanza is a dramatic interval in a narrative poem; Milton's is a narrative epilogue to a dramatic poem.

100. Abrams, "Five Types of *Lycidas*," 226.

101. Smith, *By Mourning Tongues*, 27.

102. William B. Madsen, "Voice of Michael."

103. Nelson, *Baroque Lyric Poetry*, 151.

104. Graves, "The Ghost of Milton," in his *The Common Asphodel*, 322-23; Muir, *John Milton*, 48-49; Tillyard, *Milton*, 79-85; Abrams, "Five Types of *Lycidas*," 226.

105. Smith, *Poetic Closure*, 194 n. 55.

106. Friedman, "Swain's Paideia," 5.

107. Berkeley, *Inwrought with Figures Dim*, 12, 31-32.

108. Fish, "A Poem Finally Anonymous," 328.

109. Hunt, *Italian Critics*, 145.

110. Nelson, *Baroque Lyric Poetry*, 71.

111. Fish, "A Poem Finally Anonymous," 321.

112. Martz, "Who is Lycidas?" 187.

113. Friedman, "Swain's Paideia," 8.

114. Fish, "A Poem Finally Anonymous," 339-40.

115. Martz, "Who is Lycidas?" 187. Curiously enough, F.T. Prince does not mention this aspect of the question in his study, *The Italian Element in Milton's Verse*. The basic verse pattern of *Lycidas*, he argues, is an adaptation of the Italian *canzone*, which he defines as "a complex fully rhymed stanza of some length, repeated several times, and followed by a short concluding stanza, the *commiato*." The final *ottava rima*, he believes, "undoubtedly corresponds in its own way to a *commiato*" (72-73, 120). But a *commiato* rarely, if ever, had the rhyme scheme of an *ottava rima*—the example Prince cites from Guarini's *Pastor Fido*, for instance, is in rhyming couplets.

116. Indeed, Tasso argues in his dialogue, *La Cavaletta*, that the *ottava rima*, being regular, is "less suited to lamentation" than less regular forms (quoted in Hunt, *Italian Critics*, 119).

117. Hill, *John Milton*, 68; Wittreich, *Visionary Poetics*, 61. Cf. Peter Sacks's observation that "it is as though Milton, in ending and describing his elegy, has already entered an epic" (*English Elegy*, 115). Shawcross offers a metaphorical reading of the entire stanza, in which he takes the final line to mean that "in the future [Milton] will engage in new kinds of poetic expression for the wide and expansive world" (*Self and the World*, 70).

118. Milton, *CW*, 3:234.

119. Milton, *CW*, 3:241.

120. I cannot agree, however, with Ellen Z. Lambert when she

associates Milton's "fresh woods" with Dante's "dark wood of experience" (*Placing Sorrow*, 181). The conclusion of *Lycidas* seems to me much more open-ended and less claustrophobic than that phrase implies. The final lines of *Paradise Lost* come closer in feeling.

121. Shawcross, *Self and the World*, 70.

122. Milton, *CW*, 12:27.

123. Milton uses the same image in *Ad Salsillum* (lines 9-11) to describe his departure for Italy.

Conclusion

1. Thyer, quoted in Hunter, "Obedience of Christ," 68.

2. Milton, *CW*, 15:315-16. The English translation might suggest that Christ performs one of these actions (presumably the payment of the required price by means of his crucifixion) in his divine capacity, the other (the fulfillment of the law by his rejection of Satan's temptations) in his human capacity. However, the original Latin makes it clear that Christ performed both actions in his twofold capacity of God and man: "Satisfactio est qua Christus theanthropos legem implendo iustumque pretium solvendo, divinae iustitiae pro omnibus plene satisfecit."

3. Hunter argues that Milton's doctrine of the redemption is based on the distinction between Christ's active obedience, exhibited by his life on earth, and his passive obedience, exhibited by his sacrifice on the cross (Hunter, "Obedience of Christ," 67-75). In literary, if not theological, terms, it seems to me on the contrary that Christ was essentially passive during his temptation in the desert and active during his voluntary self-sacrifice at Calvary.

4. Milton, *CW*, 15:317-18.

5. Hughes, "Christ of *Paradise Regained*." See also Frank Kermode, "Milton's Hero."

6. See, for instance, W.W. Robson, "The Better Fortitude."

7. Frye, "Typology of *Paradise Regained*," 439.

8. Guillory, "The Father's House."

9. Samuel Johnson, *Rambler* 139. Cf. Stanley Fish, "Question and Answer."

10. Barker, "Structural and Doctrinal Pattern"; Gossman, "Milton's Samson"; Parker, *Milton's Debt*; Steadman, "Milton's Hero of Faith"; Woodhouse, "Tragic Effect."

11. Mason Tung, "Samson Impatiens," 475-76. Cf. Samuel S. Stollman's summary of the play in "Milton's Samson and the Jewish Tradition": "The confrontations with Manoa, Dalila, and Harapha are basically a regenerative process for Samson whereby he perceives his

errors and his sins and emerges from the darkness of folly and servitude to the light of wisdom and liberty" (191).

12. Gossman, "Milton's Samson," 535-36, 540. Cf. Michael Atkinson's "The Structure of the Temptations in Milton's *Samson Agonistes*": "each of the three confrontations forces Samson to choose between right and wrong, and, in fact, urges him to choose the wrong. The confrontations may, therefore, legitimately be referred to as temptations" (285). More recent critics, however, either put quotation marks around the word "temptation," as Gregory F. Goekjian does in "Suicide and Revenge: *Samson Agonistes* and the Law of the Father" (258), or use some other term to describe Samson's encounters with his visitors—Burton J. Weber, for instance, calls them "opportunities for self-correction" ("Worldly End of *Samson*," 289, 296).

13. Hill, *John Milton*, 162. Cf. Don Cameron Allen's comment in *The Harmonious Vision:* "By implying that God has no further use for Samson, [Manoa] presses his son against the sharp blade of despair" (86).

14. Empson, *Milton's God*, chapter 6.

15. Samuel, "*Samson Agonistes* as Tragedy," 249. Virginia Mollenkott poses a similar question, asking, "What good is in it for Dalila? If her object were to break her husband, he is already broken. . . . why should she seek to spend the rest of her life playing nursemaid to a blind giant?" ("Relativism in *Samson Agonistes*," 94).

16. Mollenkott, "Relativism in *Samson Agonistes*," 95.

17. Gossman, "Milton's Samson," 536; Atkinson, "Structure of the Temptations," 291.

18. Krouse, *Milton's Samson*.

19. Wilkes, "Interpretation of *Samson Agonistes*"; Samuel, "*Samson Agonistes* as Tragedy"; Wittreich, *Interpreting Samson Agonistes*.

20. Wittreich, *Interpreting Samson Agonistes*, 80, 326.

21. Milton, *CW*, 7:219.

22. Milton, *CW*, 7:217-19.

23. See the introduction.

24. Aristotle, *Poetics*, in *Aristotle's Theory of Poetry and Fine Art*, trans. H.S. Butcher, 7.

25. Wilkes, "Interpretation of *Samson Agonistes*," 378.

26. Wilkes, "Interpretation of *Samson Agonistes*," 366; Tung, "Samson Impatiens," 485-86.

27. Wilkes, "Interpretation of *Samson Agonistes*," 378.

28. See Dennis Danielson, *Milton's Good God*, 82-91.

BIBLIOGRAPHY

PRIMARY SOURCES

Aristotle. *Nichomachean Ethics.* Trans. Martin Ostwald. Indianapolis: Bobbs-Merrill, 1972.

———. *Poetics.* In *Aristotle's Theory of Poetry and Fine Art,* trans. H.S. Butcher. London: Macmillan, 1932.

Auden, W.H. "In Memory of W.B. Yeats." In *Collected Shorter Poems.* London: Faber and Faber, 1950.

Augustine. *On Christian Doctrine.* Trans. D.W. Robertson Jr. New York: Bobbs-Merrill, 1958.

Bacon, Sir Francis. *The Works.* Ed. J. Spedding et al. 10 vols. Boston: Brown and Taygard, 1860-64.

Bersuirre, Pierre. *Metamorfosis Ovidiana moraliter explanata.* London, 1342.

Bidle, John. *Virgil's Bucolicks Englished.* London, 1634.

Boethius. *The Consolation of Philosophy.* Trans. Richard Green. Indianapolis: Bobbs-Merrill, 1962.

Brinsley, John. *Virgil's Eclogues . . . Translated Grammatically.* London, 1620.

Castiglione, Baldasarre. *The Book of the Courtier.* Trans. Charles S. Singleton. Garden City, N.Y.: Anchor, 1959.

Cooper, Thomas. *Dictionarium Historicum et Poeticum.* London, 1565.

Dante. *The Comedy of Dante Alighieri.* Trans. Dorothy L. Sayers. London: Penguin, 1949-62.

Donne, John. "The Canonization." In *The Elegies and the Songs and Sonnets,* ed. Helen Gardner. Oxford: Clarendon, 1965.

———. "Nativitie." In *John Donne: The Divine Poems,* ed. Helen Gardner. Oxford: Clarendon, 1952.

———. *A Sermon . . . Preach'd to the Honourable Company of the Virginia Plantation, 13 November, 1622.* London, 1622.

Dunbar, William. "Rorate caeli desuper." In *The Poems of William Dunbar,* ed. W. Mackay MacKenzie. Edinburgh: Porpoise, 1932.

Eburne, Richard. *A Plaine Pathway to Plantations.* London, 1624.

Eliot, T.S. "Journey of the Magi." In *Collected Poems 1909-1935.* London: Faber and Faber, 1936.

Farnaby, Thomas. *Publii Virgilii Maronis Bucolica, Georgica, Aeneis, Notis admarginalibus illustrata a Thoma Farnabio.* London, 1634.

Fleming, Abraham. *The Bucolicks of Publius Virgilius Maro . . . All newly Translated into English verse by Abraham Fleming.* London, 1589.

Fletcher, Giles. *Christs Victorie and Triumph.* Ed. F.S. Boas. Cambridge: Cambridge Univ. Press, 1908-9.

Herbert, George. "Christmas." In *The Works of George Herbert,* ed. F.E. Hutchinson. Oxford: Clarendon, 1941.

Herrick, Robert. "Christmas Carroll." In *Complete Poems of Robert Herrick,* ed. Alexander B. Grosart. London: Chatto and Windus, 1876.

Jonson, Ben. "A Hymne on the Nativitie of my Saviour." In *Ben Jonson: Works,* ed. C.H. Herford and Percy Simpson. Oxford: Clarendon, 1954.

Lisle, William. *Virgil's Eclogues Translated into English by W.L. Gent.* London, 1628.

Melanchthon, Philip. *Argumenta seu Dispositiones Rhetoricae in Eclogas Virgilii Authore Philip Melanchthon.* 1568.

Milton, John. *The Works of John Milton.* Gen. ed. Frank Allen Patterson. 18 vols. New York: Columbia Univ. Press, 1931-38.

———. *John Milton: Complete Poems and Major Prose.* Ed. Merritt Y. Hughes. New York: Odyssey, 1957.

More, Sir Thomas. *Utopia.* Trans. H.V.S. Ogden. New York: Appleton, Century, Crofts, 1949.

Ovid. *Metamorphoses.* Trans. M.M. Innes. London: Penguin, 1955.

Pareus, David. *Commentary Upon the Divine Revelation of the Apostle and Evangelist John.* Trans. Elias Arnold. Amsterdam, 1644.

Phillips, Edward. *The New World of English Words.* London, 1658.

Plato. *Phaedo.* Trans. F.J. Church. Indianapolis: Bobbs-Merrill, 1951.

Prudentius. *Apotheosis.* Trans. H.J. Thomson. Vol. 1. London: Loeb Classical Library, 1949.

Purchas, Samuel. *Purchas His Pilgrimes.* London, 1625.

Ramus, Peter. *P. Virgilii Maronis Bucolica P. Rami Professoris Regii, praelectionibus exposita.* 4th ed. Frankfurt, 1582.

Riccius, Stephanus. *Paraphrases, Ecphrases, succintae questiones, & brevia Scholia Textus in easdem Eclogas Authore M. Stephano Riccio.* 1568.

Ross, Alexander. *Mystagogus Poeticus.* London, 1647.

Ruskin, John. "Mornings in Florence." In *The Art Criticism of John Ruskin,* ed. Robert L. Herbert. Garden City, N.Y.: Anchor, 1964.

Sandys, George. *Ovid's Metamorphoses Englished, Mythologiz'd and Represented in Figures.* Oxford, 1632.

Servius. *In Vergilii Bucolica et Georgica commentarii.* Ed. G. Thilo. Lipsiae, 1887.

Southwell, Robert. "New Heaven: New Warre." In *The Poems of Robert Southwell, S.J.,* ed. James H. McDonald and Nancy P. Brown. Oxford: Clarendon, 1967.

Theocritus. *Idyls I* and *VII.* In *The Pastoral Elegy,* by Thomas P. Harrison. Austin: Univ. of Texas Press, 1939.

Vaughan, Henry. "Christ's Nativity." In *The Works of Henry Vaughan,* ed. L.C. Martin. 2d ed. Oxford: Clarendon, 1957.

Virgil. *Eclogues.* In *Virgil with an English Translation,* ed. H.R. Fairclough. Cambridge: Harvard Univ. Press, 1967.

———. *Publii Virgilii Maronis Mantuani opera.* London, 1535.

———. *P. Virgilii Maronis Opera . . . cum xi acerrimi iudicii virorum commentariis.* Venice, 1544.

———. *P. Vergilii Maronis Bucolica Cum commentariis Richardi Gorraei Parisiensis.* Venice, 1554.

Vives, Juan Luis. *Io Ludovico Vivis in Bucolica Vergilii Interpretatio, Potissimum Allegorica.* Milan, 1539.

White, John. *The Planter's Plea.* London, 1630.

SECONDARY SOURCES

Abrams, M.H. "Five Types of *Lycidas.*" In *Lycidas: The Tradition and the Poem,* ed. C.A. Patrides, 216-35. Columbia: Univ. of Missouri Press, 1983.

Adams, H.H. "The Development of the Flower Passage in *Lycidas.*" *Modern Language Notes* 45 (1950): 468-72.

Adams, Richard P. "The Archetypal Pattern of Death and Rebirth in *Lycidas.*" In *Lycidas: The Tradition and the Poem,* ed. C.A. Patrides, 111-16. Columbia: Univ. of Missouri Press, 1983.

Adams, Robert M. *Ikon: John Milton and the Modern Critics.* Ithaca: Cornell Univ. Press, 1955.

Allen, Don Cameron. *The Harmonious Vision.* Baltimore: Johns Hopkins Univ. Press, 1954.

———. *Mysteriously Meant.* Baltimore: Johns Hopkins Univ. Press, 1970.

Alpers, Paul. "The Eclogue Tradition and the Nature of Pastoral." *College English* 34 (1972/73): 352-71.

———. *The Singer of the Eclogues.* Berkeley: Univ. of California Press, 1979.

Arthos, John. "Milton, Ficino, and the *Charmides.*" *Studies in the Renaissance* 6 (1959): 261-74.

Atkinson, Michael. "The Structure of the Temptations in Milton's *Samson Agonistes.*" *Modern Philology* 69 (1972): 285-91.

Barker, Arthur E. *Milton and the Puritan Dilemma, 1640-1661.* Toronto: Univ. of Toronto Press, 1942.

————. *Milton: Modern Essays in Criticism.* New York: Oxford Univ. Press, 1965.

————. "The Pattern of Milton's *Nativity Ode.*" *University of Toronto Quarterly* 10 (1941): 167-81.

————. "Structural and Doctrinal Pattern in Milton's Later Poems." In *Essays in English Literature from the Renaissance to the Victorian Age Presented to A.S.P. Woodhouse,* ed. Millar MacLure and F.W. Watt, 169-94. Toronto: Univ. of Toronto Press, 1964.

Battestin, M.C. "John Crowe Ransom and *Lycidas,* a Reappraisal." *College English* 17 (1955/56): 223-38.

Belsey, Catherine. *John Milton: Language, Gender, Power.* Oxford: Blackwell, 1988.

Bennett, Joan S. "A Reading of *Samson Agonistes.*" In *The Cambridge Companion to Milton,* ed. Dennis Danielson, 225-41. Cambridge: Cambridge Univ. Press, 1989.

————. *Reviving Liberty: Radical Christian Humanism in Milton's Great Poems.* Cambridge: Harvard Univ. Press, 1989.

Berkeley, David. *Inwrought with Figures Dim.* The Hague: Mouton, 1974.

Bloom, Harold. *The Anxiety of Influence.* New York: Oxford Univ. Press, 1973.

Breasted, Barbara. "*Comus* and the Castlehaven Scandal." *Milton Studies* 3 (1971): 201-24.

Brooks, Cleanth and John E. Hardy, eds. *The Poems of Mr. John Milton: the 1645 Edition with Essays in Analysis.* New York: Columbia Univ. Press, 1957.

Brown, Cedric C. *John Milton's Aristocratic Entertainments.* Cambridge: Cambridge Univ. Press, 1985.

Bush, Douglas. *Mythology and the Renaissance Tradition in English Poetry.* New York: W.W. Norton, 1957.

Cain, Thomas H. "Spenser and the Renaissance Orpheus." *University of Toronto Quarterly* 41 (1971): 24-47.

Carey, John. *Poems of John Milton.* Harlow, Essex: Longmans, 1968.

Christianson, Paul. *Reformers and Babylon: English Apocalyptic Visions from the Reformation to the Eve of the Civil War.* Toronto: Univ. of Toronto Press, 1978.

Christopher, Georgia B. *Milton and the Science of the Saints*. Princeton: Princeton Univ. Press, 1982.

Condee, Ralph. W. *Structure in Milton's Poetry*. University Park, Penn.: Pennsylvania State Univ. Press, 1974.

Creaser, John. "Milton's *Comus:* The Irrelevance of the Castlehaven Scandal." *Notes and Queries* 31 (1984): 307-17.

Cullen, Patrick J. "Imitation and Metamorphosis: The Golden Age Eclogue in Spenser, Milton, and Marvell." *PMLA* 84 (1969): 1559-70.

Daiches, David. *Milton*. London: Hutchinson Univ. Library, 1957.

Daniells, Roy. *Milton, Mannerist and Baroque*. Toronto: Univ. of Toronto Press, 1963.

Danielson, Dennis. *Milton's Good God*. Cambridge: Cambridge Univ. Press, 1982.

Davidson, C. "The Young Milton, Orpheus, and Poetry." *English Studies* 59 (1978): 27-34.

Demaray, John G. *Milton and the Masque Tradition*. Cambridge: Harvard Univ. Press, 1968.

Diekhoff, John S., ed. *A Maske at Ludlow: Essays on Milton's "Comus"*. Cleveland: Case Western Reserve Univ. Press, 1968.

Dobbins, Austin C. *Milton and the Book of Revelation: The Heavenly Cycle*. University, Ala.: Univ. of Alabama Press, 1975.

DuRocher, Richard. *Milton and Ovid*. Ithaca: Cornell Univ. Press, 1985.

Dyson, A.E. "The Interpretation of *Comus*." In *A Maske at Ludlow*, ed. John Diekhoff, 102-25. Cleveland: Case Western Reserve Univ. Press, 1968.

Eagleton, Terry. *Marxism and Literary Criticism*. Berkeley and Los Angeles: Univ. of California Press, 1976.

Empson, William. *Milton's God*. London: Chatto and Windus, 1961.

———. *Some Versions of Pastoral*. Norfolk, Conn.: New Directions, 1960.

Evans, J. Martin. "Lycidas and the Dolphins." *Notes and Queries*, n.s., 25 (1978) 15-17.

———. "Lycidas, Daphnis, and Gallus." In *English Renaissance Studies Presented to Dame Helen Gardner*, ed. John Carey, 228-44. Oxford: Clarendon, 1980.

———. *The Road From Horton*. Victoria, B.C.: Victoria Univ. Press, 1983.

Fish, Stanley. "*Lycidas:* A Poem Finally Anonymous." In *Lycidas: The Tradition and the Poem*, ed. C.A. Patrides, 319-40. Columbia: Univ. of Missouri Press, 1983.

———. "Question and Answer in *Samson Agonistes*." *Critical Quarterly* 9 (1969): 237-64.

Fixler, Michael. *Milton and the Kingdoms of God*. London: Faber and Faber, 1964.

Fletcher, Angus. *The Transcendental Masque: An Essay on Milton's "Comus."* Ithaca: Cornell Univ. Press, 1971.

Fraser, G.S. "Approaches to *Lycidas*." In *The Living Milton*, ed. Frank Kermode, 32-54. London: Routledge and Kegan Paul, 1960.

French, J.M. "The Digressions in Milton's *Lycidas*." *Studies in Philology* 50 (1953): 485-90.

Friedman, Donald. M. "*Lycidas* and the Swain's Paideia." In *Lycidas: The Tradition and the Poem*, ed. C.A. Patrides, 281-302. Columbia: Univ. of Missouri Press, 1983.

Friedman, J.B. *Orpheus in the Middle Ages*. Cambridge: Harvard Univ. Press, 1970.

Fry, Paul H. *The Poet's Calling in the English Ode*. New Haven: Yale Univ. Press, 1980.

Frye, Northrop. "Literature as Context: Milton's *Lycidas*." In *Lycidas: The Tradition and the Poem*, ed. C.A. Patrides, 204-15. Columbia: Univ. of Missouri Press, 1983.

———. "The Typology of *Paradise Regained*." In *Milton: Modern Essays in Criticism*, ed. Arthur E. Barker, 429-46. New York: Oxford Univ. Press, 1965.

Goekjian, Gregory F. "Suicide and Revenge: *Samson Agonistes* and the Law of the Father." *Milton Studies* 26 (1990): 253-70.

Gossman, Ann. "Milton's Samson as the Tragic Hero Purified by Trial." *Journal of English and Germanic Philology* 61 (1962): 528-41.

Graves, Robert. *The Common Asphodel*. London: Hamish Hamilton, 1949.

Grenander, M.E. "*Samson's* Middle: Aristotle and Dr. Johnson." *University of Toronto Quarterly* 24 (1955): 377-89.

Grierson, Herbert. *First Half of the Seventeenth Century*. Edinburgh: W. Blackwood and Sons, 1906.

Guillory, John. "The Father's House: *Samson Agonistes* in Its Historical Moment." In *Re-Membering Milton: Essays on the Texts and Traditions*, ed. Mary Nyquist and Margaret W. Ferguson, 148-76. New York: Methuen, 1987.

Halpern, Richard. "The Great Instauration: Imaginary Narratives in Milton's 'Nativity Ode.'" In *Re-Membering Milton: Essays on the Texts and Traditions*, ed. Mary Nyquist and Margaret W. Ferguson, 3-24. New York: Methuen, 1987.

Hanford, J.H. "The Pastoral Elegy and Milton's *Lycidas*." In *Lycidas: The Tradition and the Poem*, ed. C.A. Patrides, 31-59. Columbia: Univ. of Missouri Press, 1983.

Harding, Davis P. *Milton and the Renaissance Ovid.* Urbana: Univ. of Illinois Press, 1946.

Hawkins, Sherman H. "Samson's Catharsis." *Milton Studies* 2 (1970): 211-30.

Herford, C.H. *The Post-War Mind of Germany.* Manchester: John Rylands Library, 1926.

Hill, Christopher. *The Experience of Defeat: Milton and Some Contemporaries.* London: Faber and Faber, 1984.

Hill, John Spencer. *John Milton: Poet, Priest, Prophet.* London: Macmillan, 1979.

Hollander, John. *The Untuning of the Sky.* Princeton: Princeton Univ. Press, 1961.

Hone, Ralph. "The Pilot of the Galilean Lake." *Studies in Philology* 56 (1959): 55-61.

Hughes, Merritt Y. "The Christ of *Paradise Regained* and the Renaissance Heroic Tradition." *Studies in Philology* 35 (1938): 254-77.

Hunt, Clay. *Lycidas and the Italian Critics.* New Haven: Yale Univ. Press, 1979.

Hunter, William B. "The Obedience of Christ in *Paradise Regained.*" In *Calm of Mind*, ed. Joseph A. Wittreich, 67-75. Cleveland: Case Western Reserve Univ. Press, 1971.

Jacobs, Laurence H. "'Unexpressive Notes': The Decorum of Milton's *Nativity Ode.*" *Essays in Literature* 1 (1974): 166-77.

James, William. *The Varieties of Religious Experience.* New York: Modern Library, 1936.

Jayne, Sears. "The Subject of Milton's Ludlow Mask." *PMLA* 74 (1959): 533-43.

Johnson, Samuel. *Rambler* 139. Introduction by Sidney Roberts. London: Dent, 1963.

Kastor, Frank. "Miltonic Narration: Christ's Nativity." *Anglia* 86 (1968): 339-52.

Kendrick, Christopher. "Milton and Sexuality: A Symptomatic Reading of *Comus.*" In *Re-Membering Milton: Essays on the Texts and Traditions*, ed. Mary Nyquist and Margaret W. Ferguson, 43-73. New York: Methuen, 1987.

Kermode, Frank. "Milton's Hero." *Review of English Studies* 4 (1953): 317-30.

———, ed. *The Living Milton.* London: Routledge and Kegan Paul, 1960.

Kerrigan, William. "The Irrational Coherence of *Samson Agonistes.*" *Milton Studies* 22 (1986): 217-32.

———. *The Prophetic Milton.* Charlottesville: Univ. Press of Virginia, 1974.

————. *The Sacred Complex: On the Psychogenesis of "Paradise Lost."* Cambridge: Harvard Univ. Press, 1983.

Keynes, Geoffrey, ed. *On the Morning of Christ's Nativity: Milton's Hymn with Illustrations by William Blake.* Cambridge: Cambridge Univ. Press, 1923.

Kirkconnell, Watson. *Awake the Courteous Echo.* Toronto: Univ. of Toronto Press, 1973.

Kristeller, Paul Oskar. *Renaissance Thought.* New York: Harper Torchbooks, 1955.

Krouse, Michael. *Milton's Samson and the Christian Tradition.* Princeton: Princeton Univ. Press, 1949.

Lambert, Ellen Zetzel. *Placing Sorrow: A Study of the Pastoral Elegy Convention from Theocritus to Milton.* Univ. of North Carolina Studies in Comparative Literature, no. 60. Chapel Hill: Univ. of North Carolina Press, 1976.

Landy, Marcia. "Language and the Seal of Silence in *Samson Agonistes.*" *Milton Studies* 2 (1970): 175-94.

Lawry, Jon. *The Shadow of Heaven.* Ithaca: Cornell Univ. Press, 1968.

Leach, Edmund. *Culture and Communication.* Cambridge: Cambridge Univ. Press, 1976.

LeComte, Edward S. "Sly Milton: The Meaning Lurking in the Contexts of his Quotations." *Greyfriar* 19 (1978): 3-28.

————. *Yet Once More: Verbal and Psychological Pattern In Milton.* New York: Liberal Arts, 1953.

Leonard, John. "Milton's Vow of Celibacy: A Reconsideration of the Evidence." In *Of Poetry and Politics: New Essays on Milton and His World,* ed. P.G. Stanwood, 187-201. Binghamton, N.Y.: Medieval and Renaissance Texts and Studies, 1995.

Levinson, Daniel J. *The Seasons of a Man's Life.* New York: Ballantine, 1979.

Lieb, Michael. "Milton and the Kenotic Christology: Its Literary Bearing." *ELH* 37 (1970): 342-60.

————. "'Yet Once More': The Formulaic Opening of *Lycidas.*" *Milton Quarterly* 12 (1978): 23-28.

Lochman, Daniel T. "'Seeking Just Occasion': Law, Reason and Justice at Samson's Peripety." *Milton Studies* 26 (1990): 271-88.

Loewenstein, David. *Milton and the Drama of History: Historical Vision, Iconoclasm, and the Literary Imagination.* Cambridge: Cambridge Univ. Press, 1990.

Lovejoy, Arthur O. *The Great Chain of Being.* New York: Harper and Row, 1960.

Macklem, Michael. "Love, Nature, and Grace in Milton." *Queen's Quarterly* 56 (1949): 534-47.

MacLaren, I.S. "Milton's *Nativity Ode:* The Function of Poetry and Structures of Response in 1629." *Milton Studies* 15 (1981): 181-200.

Maddison, Carol. *Apollo and the Nine: A History of the Ode.* London: Johns Hopkins Univ. Press, 1960.

Madsen, William B. "The Idea of Nature in Milton's Poetry." In *Three Studies in the Renaissance: Sydney, Jonson, Milton,* by William B. Madsen, 181-283. New Haven: Yale Univ. Press, 1958.

———. "The Voice of Michael in *Lycidas.*" *Studies in English Literature* 3 (1963): 1-7.

Marcus, Leah S. "The Milieu of Milton's *Comus:* Judicial Reform at Ludlow and the Problem of Sexual Assault." *Criticism* 25 (1983): 293-327.

Martin, Jeanne. "Transformation of Genre in Milton's *Comus.*" *Genre* 20 (1978): 195-213.

Martindale, Andrew, and Edi Baccheschi. *The Complete Paintings of Giotto.* New York: Harry N. Abrams, 1966.

Martz, Louis L. "Who is Lycidas?" *Yale French Studies* 47 (1972): 170-88.

Mayerson, Caroline W. "The Orpheus Image in *Lycidas.*" In *Lycidas: The Tradition and the Poem,* ed. C.A. Patrides, 116-28. Columbia: Univ. of Missouri Press, 1983.

Mayor, Joseph B. *Virgil's Messianic Eclogue.* London: J. Murray, 1907.

McGuire, Maryann. *Milton's Puritan Masque.* Athens: Univ. of Georgia Press, 1983.

Meier, T.K. "Milton's *Nativity Ode:* Sectarian Discord." *Modern Language Review* 65 (1970): 7-10.

Miles, Josephine. "The Primary Language of *Lycidas.*" In *Lycidas: The Tradition and the Poem,* ed. C.A. Patrides, 86-91. Columbia: Univ. of Missouri Press, 1983.

Mollenkott, Virginia R. "Relativism in *Samson Agonistes.*" *Studies in Philology* 68 (1970): 89-102.

Morris, David B. "Drama and Stasis in Milton's *Ode on the Morning of Christ's Nativity.*" *Studies in Philology* 68 (1971): 207-22.

Muir, Kenneth. *John Milton.* London: Longmans, Green and Co., 1960.

Nelson, Lowry. *Baroque Lyric Poetry.* New Haven: Yale Univ. Press, 1961.

Nicolson, Marjorie H. *John Milton.* New York: Columbia Univ. Press, 1963.

Nock, A.D. *Conversion.* Oxford: Clarendon, 1933.

Norbrook, David. *Poetry and Politics in the English Renaissance.* London: Routledge and Kegan Paul, 1984.

Nyquist, Mary, and Margaret W. Ferguson, eds. *Re-Membering Milton: Essays on the Texts and Traditions.* New York: Methuen, 1987.

Ogilvie, R.M. "The Song of Thyrsis." *Journal of Hellenic Studies* 82 (1962): 106-10.

Parker, Patricia. *Inescapable Romance: Studies in the Poetics of a Mode.* Princeton: Princeton Univ. Press, 1986.

Parker, W.R. *Milton's Debt to Greek Tragedy.* Baltimore: Johns Hopkins Univ. Press, 1937.

Patrides, C.A. "The Cessation of the Oracles: The History of a Legend." *Modern Language Review* 60 (1965): 500-507.

——, ed. *Lycidas: The Tradition and the Poem.* Columbia: Univ. of Missouri Press, 1983.

Patrides, C.A., and Joseph Wittreich, eds. *The Apocalypse in English Renaissance Thought and Literature: Patterns, Antecedents and Repercussions.* Ithaca: Cornell Univ. Press, 1984.

Patterson, Annabel, ed. *John Milton.* Harlow, Essex: Longmans, 1992.

Prince, F.T. *The Italian Element in Milton's Verse.* Oxford: Clarendon, 1954.

Putnam, Michael C.J. *Virgil's Pastoral Art.* Princeton: Princeton Univ. Press, 1970.

Radzinowicz, Mary Ann. *Toward Samson Agonistes: The Growth of Milton's Mind.* Princeton: Princeton Univ. Press, 1978.

Rajan, Balachandra. "In Order Serviceable." *Modern Language Review* 3 (1968): 13-22.

——. *The Lofty Rhyme.* Coral Gables, Fla.: Univ. of Miami Press, 1970.

——. "*Lycidas:* The Shattering of the Leaves." *Studies in Philology* 64 (1967): 51-64.

——. *The Prison and the Pinnacle.* Toronto: Univ. of Toronto Press, 1973.

Rand, E.K. "Milton in Rustication." *Studies in Philology* 19 (1922): 109-35.

Ransom, John Crowe. "A Poem Nearly Anonymous." In *Lycidas: The Tradition and the Poem,* ed. C.A. Patrides, 68-85. Columbia: Univ. of Missouri Press, 1983.

Reesing, John. *Milton's Poetic Art.* Cambridge: Harvard Univ. Press, 1968.

Richardson, Alan, ed. *A Dictionary of Christian Theology.* Philadelphia: Westminster, 1969.

Riley, Joanne M. "Milton's Lycidas: New Light on the Title." *Notes and Queries* 24 (1977): 545.

Robson, Wallace. "The Better Fortitude." In *The Living Milton,* ed.

Frank Kermode, 124-37. London: Routledge and Kegan Paul, 1960.

Rollinson, Philip. "Milton's Nativity Poem and the Decorum of Genre." *Milton Studies* 7 (1975): 165-88.

Rose, H.J. *The Eclogues of Vergil.* Berkeley and Los Angeles: Univ. of California Press, 1942.

Rudrum, Alan, ed. *Milton, Modern Judgements.* London: Macmillan, 1968.

Rumrich, John P. *Milton Unbound.* Cambridge: Cambridge Univ. Press, 1996.

Sacks, Peter M. *The English Elegy: Studies in the Genre from Spenser to Yeats.* Baltimore: Johns Hopkins Univ. Press, 1985.

Samuel, Irene. "*Samson Agonistes* as Tragedy." In *Calm of Mind*, ed. Joseph A. Wittreich, 235-57. Cleveland: Case Western Reserve Univ. Press, 1971.

Schwartz, Regina M. *Remembering and Repeating: Biblical Creation in Paradise Lost.* Cambridge: Cambridge Univ. Press, 1988.

Shafer, Robert. *The English Ode to 1660: An Essay in Literary History.* Princeton: Princeton Univ. Press, 1918.

Shawcross, John T. "Certain Relations of the MSS. of *Comus*." *Publications of the Bibliographical Society of America* 54 (1960): 35-56, 293-94.

―――. "Irony as Tragic Effect: *Samson Agonistes* and the Tragedy of Hope." In *Calm of Mind*, ed. Joseph A. Wittreich, 289-306. Cleveland: Case Western Reserve Univ. Press, 1971.

―――. *John Milton: The Self and the World.* Lexington: Univ. Press of Kentucky, 1993.

―――. "Speculations on the Dating of the Trinity MS." *Modern Language Notes* 75 (1960): 11-17.

Shuster, George N. *The English Ode from Milton to Keats.* New York: Columbia Univ. Press, 1940.

Skulsky, Harold. *Justice in the Dock: Milton's Experimental Tragedy.* Newark: Univ. of Delaware Press, 1995.

Smith, Barbara H. *Poetic Closure.* Chicago: Univ. of Chicago Press, 1968.

Smith, Eric. *By Mourning Tongues: Studies in English Elegy.* Ipswich, U.K.: Boydell, 1977.

Smith, G.W., Jr. "Milton's Revisions and the Design of *Comus*." *ELH* 46 (1979): 56-80.

―――. "Milton's Method of Mistakes in the *Nativity Ode*." *Studies in English Literature* 18 (1978): 107-23.

Sprott, S.E. *John Milton, A Maske: The Earlier Versions.* Toronto: Univ. of Toronto Press, 1973.

Stanwood, P.G., ed. *Of Poetry and Politics: New Essays on Milton and His World.* Binghamton, N.Y.: Medieval and Renaissance Texts and Studies, 1995.

Stapleton, Lawrence. "Milton and the New Music." *University of Toronto Quarterly* 23 (1954): 217-26.

Steadman, J.M. "Chaste Music and *Casta Juventus:* Milton, Minturno, and Scaliger on Inspiration and the Poet's Character." *Italica* 40 (1963): 28-34.

———. "Faithful Champion: The Theological Basis of Milton's Hero of Faith." *Anglia* 77 (1959): 12-28.

Stollman, Samuel S. "Milton's Samson and the Jewish Tradition." *Milton Studies* 3 (1971): 185-200.

Tillyard, E.M.W. *The Elizabethan World Picture.* London: Chatto and Windus, 1943.

———. *Milton.* London: Chatto and Windus, 1930.

———. *Studies in Milton.* London: Chatto and Windus, 1951.

Tung, Mason. "Samson Impatiens: A Reinterpretation of Milton's *Samson Agonistes.*" *Texas Studies in Language and Literature* 9 (1968): 475-92.

Tuve, Rosemond. *Images and Themes in Five Poems by Milton.* Cambridge: Harvard Univ. Press, 1957.

———. "Theme, Pattern, and Imagery in *Lycidas.*" In *Lycidas: The Tradition and the Poem,* ed. C.A. Patrides, 171-204. Columbia: Univ. of Missouri Press, 1983.

Tuveson, Ernest L. *Millennium and Utopia.* Berkeley and Los Angeles: Univ. of California Press, 1949.

Walker, D.P. "Orpheus the Theologian and Renaissance Platonists." *Journal of the Warburg and Courtauld Institutes* 16 (1953): 100-120.

Weber, Burton J. "The Schematic Design of the *Samson* Middle." *Milton Studies* 22 (1986): 233-54.

———. "The Worldly End of *Samson.*" *Milton Studies* 26 (1990): 289-309.

White, M.E., ed. *Studies in Honor of Gilbert Norwood.* Toronto: Univ. of Toronto Press, 1952.

Whiting, George W. *Milton and This Pendant World.* Austin: Univ. of Texas Press, 1958.

Wilding, Michael. *Dragons Teeth: Literature in the English Revolution.* Oxford: Clarendon, 1987.

Wilkes, G.A. "The Interpretation of *Samson Agonistes.*" *Huntington Library Quarterly* 26 (1963): 363-79.

Williamson, Marilyn. "The Myth of Orpheus in *L'Allegro* and *Il Penseroso.*" *Modern Language Quarterly* 32 (1971): 377-86.

Wind, Edgar. *Pagan Mysteries in the Renaissance*. London: Faber and Faber, 1968.

Wittreich, Joseph A., Jr., ed. *Calm of Mind: Tercentary Essays on "Paradise Regained" and "Samson Agonistes" in Honor of John S. Diekhoff*. Cleveland: Case Western Reserve Univ. Press, 1971.

———. *Interpreting "Samson Agonistes."* Princeton: Princeton Univ. Press, 1986.

———. *Visionary Poetics: Milton's Tradition and His Legacy*. San Marino, Calif.: Huntington Library, 1979.

Woodhouse, A.S.P. "The Argument of Milton's *Comus*." *University of Toronto Quarterly* 11 (1941): 46-71.

———. "Milton's Pastoral Monodies." In *Studies in Honor of Gilbert Norwood*, ed. M.E. White, 261-78. Toronto: Univ. of Toronto Press, 1952.

———. "Notes on Milton's Early Development." *University of Toronto Quarterly* 13 (1943): 66-101

———. "Tragic Effect in *Samson Agonistes*." *University of Toronto Quarterly* 28 (1958-59): 205-22.

Woodhouse, A.S.P., and Douglas Bush, eds. *A Variorum Commentary on the Poems of John Milton*. 6 vols. Gen. ed. Merritt Y. Hughes. New York: Columbia Univ. Press, 1970-.

INDEX

abstinence, 43; chastity and, 70; conflict with temperance, 54–58; doctrine of the mean and, 58–61; in redemption, 121, 122, 123. *See also* celibacy; virginity

activism, 9

Adam: in *Paradise Lost*, 130; temperance and, 55–56

Adonis (Fletcher the Elder), 141–42 n 15

Ad Patrem (Milton), 86–87, 98, 104, 115, 143–44 n 36

Aeropagitica (Milton), 61, 66

L'Allegro (Milton), 5, 9, 86

allusion: in *Lycidas*, 76

Amaryllis, 82, 93–94

America, 25

angels, 66

Anglicanism: banishment and, 26

anonymity, 12–13

Apollo. *See* Phoebus Apollo

An Apology Against a Pamphlet (Milton), 59

Apology for Smectymnuus (Milton), 104, 105

apotheosis: in *Lycidas*, 103–6

Arethusa, 82

Aristotle: on drama, 128–129; on virtue, 44

Arnulf of Orleans, 90

At a Solemn Music (Milton), 104

Attendant Spirit (character in *Comus*): as grace, 68–69; as humanist educator, 65–66

Aubade, 35

Augustine, Saint, 21–22, 30–31

autobiography: *Lycidas* and, 72, 110–11; in *On the Morning of Christ's Nativity*, 11–13; in *Samson Agonistes*, 123–24

awakening, 2–3

bacchanal, 106

Bacchantes, 76, 86, 143 n 34

banishment: in English Renaissance, 24–26; theological implications of, 29–30. *See also* exclusion

bed, marriage, 148 n 90

"betweeness," 6, 61

Bible: convention of repetition and, 75

Boccaccio, Giovanni, 83–84, 90

Book of Revelation. *See* Revelations

The Book of the Courtier (Castiglione), 54

Bridgewater, Earl of. *See* Egerton, John

Brightman, Thomas, 7–8

Calvin, John, 32

Camus, 97

Canonization (Donne), 87